NATALIA KREINBRING

JUST Breathe

Print ISBN: 978-1-66783-983-7
eBook ISBN: 978-1-66783-984-4

Printed in the United States of America

TABLE OF CONTENTS

FOREWORD

Never in a million years did I think this story would be my story. After all, these kinds of things didn't happen to me or wouldn't happen to me. At the time Beckett was born, I was a young twenty-eight-year-old woman in excellent health. I wasn't overweight or underweight, and I was an avid runner, ate right, never used drugs, didn't smoke—healthy as a horse, as they would say.

As I look back on my short pregnancy with Beckett, I do remember my senses telling me something was wrong. You see, I feel like I've always had this sixth sense about me. This is not one of the traditional senses we all know: touch, sight, smell, etc. This was something unexplained. An aching of my heart, an intuition in my gut . . . I felt something was wrong with my baby. At one of my prenatal visits, I mentioned my prenotion that I felt something was wrong or going to be wrong with my baby. My doctor assured me everything was fine with my baby and shared with me how she had practiced with the public health department before going into private practice and that she had delivered babies whose mothers were homeless, drug addicts, in poor health, or had never had one single prenatal appointment. I was doing everything right, and by all the measurements, labs and sonograms, the baby and I were going to be just fine.

I also shared this feeling with my brother, to which he assured me, as well, all would be fine, and he would submit a prayer request to the Benedictine Sisters requesting health and safety for me and my unborn baby. I still have the letter of their watchful prayer which arrived after Beckett had been born. I remember upon opening that letter I just wanted to rip it into shreds. I was so lost, hurt, confused, emotional and angry. How? How did God let this happen? Did he not hear the prayers of the "sisters"? Did he not hear mine in my deepest and darkest hour?

Our journey with Beckett was riddled with pure bliss and absolute heartbreak, which seemed to go from one extreme to the other within a matter of moments. Looking back on it now, it's a miracle that I didn't end up in a nuthouse or needing long-term psychological drugs just to function. But that's not to say that our journey with Beckett was not life altering; it was. It still is, and it's those experiences and changes that have compelled me to share Beckett's story. Because while this is my story, it could be yours too. Unfortunately, the premature birthrate in the United States averages 9.8 percent per year, according to the March of Dimes. That means one in every ten babies will be born too soon. Because of that, so many of you might have walked, be walking or may someday walk in my shoes down this long and winding road.

I hope that in reading Beckett's story you find comfort in knowing you are not alone in your journey, whatever that journey maybe. I hope you find hope when you are hopeless and determination when the odds seem to be against you. Above all, though, I hope that you bear witness to the power of love as profoundly evident throughout the story. Not just love, but unconditional love, the kind that will carry us through the darkest of nights and in our moments of deepest despair. This is Beckett's story.

BMK

December 31st, 2010—it was unseasonably warm for it being New Year's Eve, and Ryan decided to take advantage of the warmth to go golfing for the day with friends. That evening we were planning to attend a New Year's Eve party at a friend's house just a few houses down the street from us, but I had all afternoon before I needed to get ready. For whatever reason I thought cleaning the windows in my bedroom that day was something that must be done. Mind you, at this point, I was barely twenty-six-weeks pregnant. Probably enough that I shouldn't be cleaning windows, but anyone who knows me knows my determination to get things done and knows that it doesn't allow for things to happen later when I want them done now.

So, I waddled my way up the step ladder six times over. I nearly lost circulation in my fingers as I pulled the cord of the blinds until they cleared the window panel, allowing me to spray the cleaner and wipe them clean. I finished, showered and waited for Ryan to get home so we could head to the bowling alley where our party for the night was starting. I remember a dull ache in my back and in general sick feeling in my stomach. I chalked it up to doing too much for the day, or maybe this was how one feels when they are about to enter the third trimester of pregnancy. After all, this was my first pregnancy, and so maybe this was the norm I should come to expect. We headed to the bowling alley, and I proceeded to throw an eight-pound ball down the lane a few times. Probably not the grandest idea, but up until this point, all was going well with the pregnancy, so why would I

3

even second guess that? However, I couldn't shake the pain in my lower back. We headed back to our friend's house where we rang in the new year watching the ball drop in Times Square on TV. I remember thinking as the clock struck twelve, *This year is going to change my life.* What an understatement that would be.

Back home, I didn't sleep well that night. My back still ached, and my stomach did, too. I must have overdone it, I thought, or ate too much crappy finger food. I tossed and turned but didn't share my feeling of illness with Ryan as he was enjoying a bit too much alcohol-induced slumber. By morning, I felt this weird tightening of my belly. It wasn't painful, and I couldn't tell if I was going to get sick or honestly just needed to take a big crap. Around 9:00 or 10:00 a.m., with Ryan still struggling to come back to the living, I finally realized that maybe I was having contractions as I could time them out with consistency. At this point, I believe they were around nine to ten minutes apart.

I shared with Ryan what I thought was happening and proceeded to call my doctor. She thought it could just be Braxton Hicks or that my body was dehydrated. She advised me to drink at least 32 oz of water or more if possible, take two Tylenol and lie on my left side in bed and rest. I was to call her if that didn't help to stop the contractions. I actually fell asleep for a few hours, and when I awoke, I did feel better. I got up, showered and Ryan and I decided to grab some Mexican food for dinner. It was around 7:00 p.m. on Saturday and the restaurant was packed, so we decided to dine at the bar. I knew things were not right as soon as we sat down. Not only were the contractions back, but I doubled over in pain as each one surged through my body. Upon returning home, we called the doctor again who advised me to head to the hospital for observation.

Once checked in and hooked up to all the machines, they confirmed I was having contractions but was not dilated at all. That was good news. I was given IV fluids and two shots of muscle relaxants to get the contractions to stop. On the monitors, it appeared that the contractions were slowing and lessening in intensity, so around midnight, I told Ryan he might as well go home and sleep and to come back in the morning and get me. After all, there was no need for both of us to stay in the hospital and not be sleeping if all was going to be okay.

I woke up around 2:00 a.m. and had to go to the restroom. As I stood from the hospital bed, I noticed blood on the bedsheet. I froze for a moment staring in shock at what I saw and thinking maybe I was dreaming this or that was a stain or something. I touched it to make sure. I called the nurse who rushed me back to the bed and checked me. I knew things were not good when she ran into the hallway and another nurse came into the room to also check me. They both confirmed I was about 4 cm dilated. In a matter of seconds, my quiet, dark hospital room turned into a frenzy of lights, monitors, IV pumps, nurses and doctors. People were rushing in and out of my room, and all I could do was try to comprehend what was happening. I called Ryan who rushed back to the hospital while I was given additional muscle relaxing shots and pumps of magnesium via IV to try to stop the contractions or at least slow them. I remember asking one of the nurses what was going to happen to my baby. While her lips spoke words of comfort, her eyes showed me the uncertainty she was trying to hide.

My doctor arrived and checked to ensure the baby was still head down via ultrasound, which he was. She advised that I needed to be immediately transferred to Saint Luke's Hospital that had a level 3 NICU and could provide the best care for the baby after he was born. She said it was critical that I get there as soon as possible; otherwise I would deliver at Liberty Hospital and they would have to transport the baby without me to Saint Luke's, which was about a thirty-minute drive. By this point, I was still in shock about everything. *What in the hell was happening?* I was young and healthy, and everything was going great, and now? Now I was being transported in an ambulance to a hospital with a level 3 NICU where I was going to give birth to my first son fourteen weeks early! I remember asking my doctor as the transport team arrived if she was coming with me. I had no idea that doctors can't just travel from one hospital to the next

5

to treat their patents. When she told me she couldn't and held my head, planting a kiss on top, I felt the last drop of "things could still be okay" fall from the bottom of my heart. Her eyes too showed fear and uncertainty.

I was taken by ambulance to Saint Luke's Hospital right around 3:00 a.m. Despite being majorly drugged up, I remember that ambulance ride so clearly. I can still see my pregnant belly strapped into the transport bed with my hospital water cup wedged on the side. I can vividly remember the iridescent lights, sound of the chains rattling under the ambulance and feeling so alone. Ryan couldn't ride with me, and so here I was alone in labor with my first baby in an ambulance going to some hospital I had never dreamed of ever going to and I was about to deliver.

I arrived at Saint Luke's and was taken into Labor and Delivery. Thankfully, Ryan was there about the same time I was being wheeled into the room. And so we started the process of answering the doctor and nurse's questions and trying to mentally prepare ourselves for what we knew was coming. But we weren't ready for this. No one is ready for this, unless they are forty-weeks pregnant and can't wait to deliver their baby. But at twenty-six weeks, no, no one. I think that hardest part was when the NICU nurse came and spoke with us and basically told us that we needed to be prepared to make a split-second decision once the baby was born regarding how much life support we wanted to provide. I remember looking at Ryan once she left, and I think we both had a blank, numb look on our faces.

From then, it was a waiting game: 7 cm . . . 9cm . . . It was awful, waiting for something that you never wanted, ever! I don't remember speaking to Ryan during this time. I prayed over and over in my head for God's mercy to be upon my baby and me. And if he couldn't stop this train, then please God, please just keep my baby alive. Finally, at 10 cm, I was moved into the operating room and started pushing. I was able to get an epidural; however, I only received a partial block and so felt most of labor. My water broke while pushing, and it was literally like a water balloon spraying all over the room including the doctors and nurse. I was so drugged from the muscle relaxants, magnesium and epidural that it all seemed hazy, but I do remember wanting to get my baby out as quick as possible. And so I did.

On January 2, 2011, at 6:56 a.m., I delivered my son. I was so out of it by the time he emerged I remember Ryan saying, "Look, Nat, there he is!" as the doctor briefly held him up for us to see. He was *so small*, but he was crying and bright pink and I knew that was a good sign. He was there, and then he was gone, as he was rushed over to the team of NICU doctors and nurses who were awaiting his arrival. From there, I finished with the delivery process and was moved to recovery. Once I was cleared from recovery, I was taken to the NICU unit to see my son. I felt numb. Here I was looking at my 2 lbs 2 oz baby in an incubator, and all I could think was that he should still be in my belly. It felt so surreal.

I was moved to a post-delivery room where Ryan and I tried to make sense of the last twenty-four hours. All of a sudden, we were parents, parents to a very small and sick premature baby. My mom and dad arrived shortly after 10:00 a.m., and while I was glad they were there, it was hard to know the circumstances in which they had come was not a joyful one. In the afternoon, a lactation nurse came to help me start pumping for my milk. I felt like a child learning about the body for the first time.

Nurse: "Okay, you will need this size nipple shield based upon the size of your nipples."

Me: "Ahh what? There are actual sizes to nipples? So I hook up all this stuff and then I have to sit here and pump for twenty to thirty 30 minutes?" *Humm, okay ...* "Holy crap this hurts, not just my nipples, but my uterus!"

I seriously remember looking at the nurse like she had ten heads when she told me I would need to pump every two to three hours. I had no idea about any of this. I wasn't supposed to; I was still supposed to be pregnant for another three months for Pete's sake!

That night as I lay in my hospital room, my mind flashed back through the images of the day—the ambulance ride, the operating room, the incubator in the NICU—and I debated in my mind if I wanted to give our son the name I always loved knowing that there was a chance he could not make it. I think it was in that moment I knew I needed to make a difficult choice. I needed to make up my mind: I could either put every ounce of love and determination into this baby, or I could let fear win and withhold getting emotionally involved with this baby and try to protect my own heart if we lost him. That night, I chose love and determination. And that night, we named our first born "Beckett Michael Kreinbring," "BMK."

THE RIDE

The First Two Days

Beckett was born on a Sunday morning, and I was able to stay in inpatient at the hospital in the post-delivery area for two days. During those two days, I pumped and shuffled my way back and forth to the NICU to deliver milk or sit with Beckett. I can remember the first time I was taken to see Beckett after delivering him. Ryan wheeled me over in a wheelchair from my room, and upon entering Beckett's room, I just felt sick. There in the incubator, connected to a million cords and lines, was my tiny baby. He looked every bit of a newborn baby, but I desperately wanted this not to be my baby. I desperately wished to turn back time and change this. I wanted to run from the room. I wanted someone to wake me from this terrible dream. This was not the birth I imagined in my head when I learned of my pregnancy. This was not the way I planned to welcome my first born into the world. I imagined friends and family coming to visit at the hospital, showing up with flowers and balloons, and I showing with pride my brand-new baby boy. But reality was smacking me in the face with every nurse and doctor and buzzing alarm. This was real, and he was there before my eyes to validate it. That tiny and vulnerable baby boy was mine. His eyes were still fused shut, his body still covered with lanugo, his skin nearly translucent, his lungs unable to function, his body too young and week to feed. I felt so disconnected from this baby. I could do nothing for him. I couldn't hold him or feed him, I couldn't care for him, I couldn't protect

9

him—hell I couldn't even keep him alive. It was the most helpless I've ever felt in my entire life.

As I sat staring into Beckett's incubator, my thoughts were interrupted by the nurse who asked if I wanted to help with Beckett's cares. It again brought me back to the reality at hand, and I said yes, even though I had no idea what "cares" were. Tracy, who was our nurse that day, showed me how to open the holes in the incubator. She showed Ryan and I how to change Beckett's diaper, take his temperature, moved different monitors and probes to different parts of his body and change his position so that he didn't develop sores on his skin. We applied topical ointment to his skin, and I was so afraid I would rip it open as it was so paper thin. I remember freaking out when she ever so gently picked up Beckett's fragile body and repositioned him to lay on his opposite side. She did so with so much compassion and so much care, ensuring Beckett's arms and legs were just right, straightening all the cords, wires and tubes. Then she tucked him back in using rolls of blankets and other bedding to make him feel like he was still snug inside of my belly. Tracy also taught us to cradle Beckett using our hands. As we learned, the skin and nerves of a premature baby are too sensitive for "petting," so the best way to touch Beckett was to just cradle our hands around his legs and tiny head with slight pressure.

I felt overwhelmed and again helpless that this lady could take better care of my baby than I could. My heart sank, and my eyes cried. It was all too much. I settled back into my wheelchair and stared again into the incubator. Alarms started to ring, and both Ryan and I nearly jumped out of our pants thinking Beckett had stopped breathing or his heart had stopped. Calmly, Tracy walked in, checked Beckett and silenced the alarm. We were lost. We weren't idiots, but we weren't medical people either. We had no idea what the alarms meant, but we were learning. We sat in Beckett's room nearly all day everyday those first two days. Tracy continued to be Beckett's day nurse, and while my mind bucked towards anger in being faced with all of this, Tracy graced me by sharing her knowledge of preemie babies and caring for them. She said she was proud of me for keeping up with pumping milk for Beckett. She encouraged me when I was afraid of trying to perform the cares for Beckett. She handed me Kleenexes when the tears came and refilled my water when needed. She was Beckett's nurse, but in every way, she was mine too.

And so, between Tracy's teaching, the multiple tests that were being run on Beckett and the doctors who would come around and help give us status updates on Beckett's condition, a light began to shine into our future, and we slowly saw the path we would be walking. Although unlike most paths in life where you can see the destination in the far-off distance, the final destination to our path was unknown. It looked overgrown and bore thick brambles and rocks that would make it a treacherous journey. It was dark and winding only allowing for glimmers of what general direction we were to go. We weren't sure where we were headed nor where we would end up, but we knew one thing for certain now, that this was *our* path.

On the Tuesday after Beckett's birth, I was discharged from the hospital, although it felt like more of an eviction to me. I didn't want to leave. I had the smallest room in the postpartum area (since there was no baby rooming in with me), the food was terrible and I would cry at night listening to the cries of neighboring mother's babies knowing mine couldn't even be in my room with me nor could I provide for him the way they were providing to their babies. My heart sank when I would see the "Newborn pictures in progress" sign on other mothers' doors and see smiling family and friends in the hallways anxious to meet new life. Despite all that, I could walk at any time of day down two short hallways and see my baby. We weren't together, but we weren't far away either, until that day. The postpartum nurse for that day helped Ryan load up a cart with all our belongings, which included a breast pump I had to rent from the hospital as I didn't have one yet but wanted to continue to pump and store milk for Beckett. Ryan pulled up the car and loaded everything including me. I cried all the way home, and upon entering our house, I cried more. I felt guilty, like I was leaving Beckett behind, and empty, as a piece of me was still at that hospital and all I wanted to do was go back and get it and bring it home with us.

The first month

As days turned to weeks, we slowly started to navigate our way through the NICU. Anyone who's ever had a baby in the NICU, worked in the NICU or heard about the NICU knows it's always compared to one thing: a rollercoaster ride. And that it is. One moment you're over the moon as your baby just had his first bowel movement, and two seconds later, you receive a lab result saying that his blood gas report for how well his lungs are oxygenating his blood is so bad that they are needing to give him a sedative and intubate him with a breathing tube. Combine all the good news, bad news and waiting for news with multiple device alarms, and it becomes the most emotionally draining experience *ever*. Period.

And so was the case with Beckett. The first few weeks of his life in the NICU, I felt like we rode up, we rode down and we waited anxiously for news about how crazy the ride was going to get in the future. With micro-preemies, as I learned Beckett would be classified as since he was born right near twenty-six-weeks gestation, tests are run, and you wait to hear or see results on the functioning of the baby's lungs, brain, heart and gastrointestinal track. Obviously, all these are critical organs or system functions needed to sustain life. And truthfully, that was all we focused on initially, "sustaining," surviving from one minute to the next.

After discharge, I fell into a new routine since walking down the hallway for a visit or status update was no longer possible. Each day went something like this: after pumping every three hours at night to keep my milk coming for Beckett, I would wake at 6:00 a.m. to call the hospital. The nurses worked twelve-hour shifts 7:00 a.m. to 7:00 p.m., so I liked to call at 6:00 a.m. so I could speak with the night nurse and see how Beckett's night had been. From there, I would shower, get ready for the day and head to the hospital around 8:00 a.m. I would then spend the entire day in

Beckett's room, helping with his cares, talking to the doctors and trying to understand what was going on inside Beckett's body and which direction we were headed for that day, although sometimes it was just for that hour. I would pack food from home or eat at the hospital cafeteria during the day. Then around 8:00 or 9:00 p.m., once I knew who the night nurse was, and that Beckett was tucked away and resting peacefully, I would head home to sleep only to wake and do it all again the next day.

The first week after Beckett's birth test started to roll in and we took each new discovery one step at a time. As we learned quickly, even good news could turn bad at a moment's notice. Like most premature babies and some term babies, Beckett's bilirubin levels skyrocketed, resulting in phototherapy. However, within a week or so, his liver had begun to function properly, and the phototherapy light and cute little "sunshades" he wore in his incubator were gone.

One of the most positive things for Beckett, and the one thing that remained positive and without recourse, was his ability to tolerate my milk for feedings. Many premature babies develop a gastrointestinal complication called NEC (necrotizing enterocolitis), which can ultimately destroy the walls of the bowel or intestines. Thankfully, Beckett's little system was able to process my milk without complications, and I think ultimately this was what helped him get through some of his other hurdles, for my milk helped sustain his body as it fought harder battles in other areas of his body.

A few days after his birth, Beckett had his first brain scan to check for intraventricular hemorrhaging (IVH), aka brain bleeding. A very common issue seen in premature babies, especially those born more than ten weeks early, as the blood vessels in their brains are not fully developed yet. And obviously, a very scary issue to deal with if a bleed is present. He was able to pass his first scan, which was done in his first week of life, and his second one was completed ten days after his birth. I can remember wanting to cry tears of joy upon hearing the news of his brain bleeds being negative on day ten. However, that joy was quickly overshadowed with unfavorable news regarding Beckett's respiratory/cardiovascular function.

We learned through an echocardiogram performed on Beckett's heart four days after his birth that he did have PDA or patent ductus arteriosus. The ductus arteriosus is essentially a passage between the two major arteries in the heart, the aorta and the pulmonary artery. This vessel is an essential part of fetal blood circulation while in utero, but usually closes up after birth. In Beckett's case, it did not. This is usually not a huge issue in full-term babies and generally something that would close up on its own, but given Beckett's size, prematurity and undeveloped lungs, his PDA would cause great respiratory complications for him.

Within hours of being born, Beckett went from just a nasal cannula (device used to deliver supplemental oxygen or increased airflow, but noninvasive) to being fully intubated, with a breathing tube down his windpipe, on a ventilator. I remember feeling sad that he needed the additional assistance and feeling like we were moving backwards. However, I had to remind myself that he was fourteen weeks early and unfortunately did not receive any of the benefit of the steroid shots they gave me while in labor, which should have helped his lungs if they would have had time to be processed in his body. The ventilator, which was now doing the breathing for him, did allow his body to not have to work as hard as it was when on the nasal cannula.

By the end of Beckett's first week of life, his respiratory conditions had deteriorated despite multiple changes in support from a ventilator and oxygen support. He had two blood transfusions. The thought was that increasing the red blood cells might help carry oxygen throughout his body. However, no level in ventilator adjustments or blood transfusions resulted in great improvements. And another echocardiogram showed that Beckett's PDA was still present, adding to the issue as the blood flowing through the heart wasn't being oxygenated the way it should have been if the opening would have been closed. At this point, the doctors recommended we treat

Beckett's PDA using a medication called indomethacin, and we agreed. The medication was administered in three doses every twelve hours. While the medication was being administered, Beckett's feeds had to be suspended, so we were basically in a waiting period for thirty-six hours. Unfortunately, the first round of indomethacin was unsuccessful, and so they started a second round. Thirty-six hours later, another echocardiogram was completed, and it appeared from the scan that the PDA did finally close. I felt like a huge weight had been lifted off my shoulders. *Good*, I thought. *Now we can hopefully start making some advancements in being able to wean his ventilator.*

As we entered Beckett's second week of life, the weight that had been lifted came crashing back down harder than ever. Beckett's respiratory function continued to deteriorate. He was moved from a traditional ventilator to a high frequency ventilator. A high frequency ventilator essentially gives lots of little breaths within a minute, like more than two hundred. The idea is to keep the lungs open all of the time so they can receive the benefit of the assistance being administered. Some babies respond well to it; some don't. So again, we waited. The doctors noticed that Beckett was fighting the vent a bit, and so they also started to sedate Beckett using fentanyl so he wouldn't fight the ventilator so much and to allow his body to rest. Three more blood transfusions were completed, and yet the level of assistance Beckett needed from the vent continued to increase. By the end of his second week of life, his right lung was near collapsing, and he was on 100% oxygen, which is the most oxygen support that you can receive.

Upon entering Beckett's room on those days, the usually bright room with large windows on the far end that allowed the sunshine to seep inside was dark. The shades were pulled, and the large sliding glass doors that separated the room from the open area where the nurses and the doctors gathered were kept shut to keep the noise down. Even Beckett's little incubator was covered with a special blanket to keep it dark and quiet. Those days, we weren't allowed to disturb Beckett unless it was time for his cares, for when someone entered his incubator, even if to only cradle or hold him with their hands, his heart rate would drop, as well as his oxygen saturation rates. By this point in our journey, I was exhausted. Not only was I still recovering from delivery, but I was exhausted from keeping up with pumping every three hours and being at the hospital for ten twelve hours every day. On top of that, the past two weeks were marked with extreme emotional highs and lows, and now here we sat in this dark room where Beckett's conditioned showed no signs of improving.

As I sat in Beckett's dark room listening to the alarms and letting my mind run in a million different directions, I tried to have courage and be strong, but honestly, I was a mess of emotions. I was so angry at my body for going into labor and wished there was some reason to explain it. But there wasn't. While pregnant, I was doing everything right (i.e., eating healthy, doing prenatal doctors' visits, taking prenatal vitamins, etc.). And besides being early, Beckett was a healthy baby. Although my mind understood that sometimes things happen and there are no explanations, I still felt so robbed: robbed of watching my belly grow bigger and bigger and the anticipation of labor; robbed of attending baby showers and having him there with me in my belly; robbed that his arrival was not a joyous event and moment and instead was one filled with fear, stress and anxiety; robbed that friends and family couldn't visit him, that I couldn't hold him or hear him cry because he was so sick.

In addition, I hurt so deeply, a hurt I had never experienced before. It hurt when I saw another mother being discharged from the hospital with her baby in tow. I hurt as I dressed each morning and saw my maternity clothes hanging in my closet haunting me. I hurt watching Beckett struggle day in and day out just to breathe and stay alive. I hurt when I saw the exhaustion and stress on Ryan's face at the end of each day as he tried to juggle Beckett, his career and me. And on top of all of this, there was stress like none other. Not just the day-to-day stress of what was going to happen with Beckett that day, but what would happen if Beckett died. How would I ever recover? And if Beckett did survive, what would his quality of life be like? Will he have lifelong disabilities from being born so early? How would we afford all these medical expenses? The list of worries and emotional pain went on and on, and there was not one damn thing to ease or control any of them.

My thoughts were interrupted as the neonatologist for the day, Dr. Anderson, entered the dark room to provide me with an update on Beckett. I threw my worries aside and sat hopeful that he had the magic solution to fix Beckett that day. He advised that they were going to try to put Beckett back on the traditional ventilator and try some different settings to see if it might provide Beckett with any relief. The high frequency ventilator, while beneficial at keeping Beckett's lungs open, didn't allow them to reduce his oxygen levels, and prolonged exposure to high levels of oxygen had its risk. The traditional vent allowed for increased pressure. However, that too could cause damage to lung tissue with prolonged exposure. He said Beckett's oxygen saturations, which should have been in the 80 to 95 percent range, was consistently around 70 percent and would periodically dip to 50 and 60 percent, so a change was needed, and unfortunately with premature babies, there is no one solution that works for all of them. All babies are different in what they will respond to, so we would try another option and hope for some improvements.

I crumbled; silent tears streamed down my face as I tried to be strong. The past two weeks I had rode the rollercoaster ride up and down and tried to keep a positive outlook, but now I was tired and wanted to get off the ride. Dr. Anderson, who would quickly become one of my favorite neonatologists, hugged me and comforted me with some reassuring insight. The first thing that he did was praise me for pumping. He said he can understand how challenging and exhausting it can be, but noted how well Beckett was tolerating my milk and even though I couldn't be at Beckett's side 24/7, each time Beckett was being fed, a part of me was there with him comforting him and filling his belly. That thought sure helped to lessen the guilt of not being there every second of the day. I was always there with Beckett, just sometimes in another form. The second thing he said was how important it was for Beckett to rest. He noted that preterm babies need *a lot* of sleep, not just light sleep, but deep REM sleep. He noted how Beckett was in REM sleep at the moment. We watched from outside his incubator as his tiny body twitched and jerked. He turned from Beckett and looked at me and said, "What do you think Beckett is dreaming of?" I stared at him blankly as I had never even thought about it. He turned back towards Beckett and said, "I like to think that our dreams come from our experiences, and so far, Beckett's experiences have been Ryan and you—not the incubator, or NICU nurses and doctors or anything that is happening now." I thought for a moment about his words and believed they were true. Beckett had spent the majority of his existence with me, hearing my voice and Ryan's and feeling safe. When in my belly, he didn't feel pain or see bright lights or get disturbed every three hours for cares. Dr. Anderson noted, "So even though you and your husband cannot physically be here all the time for Beckett, you are always here, filling his belly and his dreams." And then he said this, which became one of the most true and greatest pieces of advice shared to me while in the NICU: "While Beckett's oxygen needs and support for survival right now are high, Beckett is not in any discomfort or disturbed by it. Sure, he gets woke up more and sees more bright lights and hears more beeps than any baby should, but he's in a deep sleep most of the time and the times when he is awake, he doesn't understand any of it. It is us, the caretakers and parents, who suffer the anxiety and worry. Beckett will have no recollection of any of this. It's the parents who carry the burden of it all."

For the first time in a long time, I felt some level of reassurance. Dr. Anderson had no magic solutions for Beckett, no magic potion that would instantly make him better right then, but he did instill in me a sense of comfort, more comfort than I had felt since January 2. We were always there with Beckett in some form, and Beckett wasn't in pain or going to remember any of this. Of course, that still didn't answer all my "what if" questions, but it provided some peace to our current situation. And as I found along our journey with Beckett, sometimes it's those little moments of hope, assurance and peace that carry you through the hard days and give you strength to face the next challenge, and so I hung on to every word from Dr. Anderson that day. I always have, and I always will.

The next two weeks were a blur of trying to balance and find the right mix of support for Beckett's respiratory needs. He had good days, and he had bad days. We switched from the high frequency ventilator back to the traditional ventilator and from fentanyl to morphine. He had two more blood transfusions, bringing the total number since birth to seven. We started to fortify his milk, which essentially meant adding calories to it, in hopes that his weight gain would continue. Beckett's weight did increase. However, we were faced with a new challenge of excess fluid in his body. Additional fluid in your body isn't a good thing especially when it makes your lungs sound "wet," adding additional complications to your already compromised respiratory function. So, the doctors ordered a medication called Lasix that essentially allowed Beckett's body to pee out the excess fluid.

Adding to the blur of these weeks was the fact that I decided to return to work. With Beckett staying in the NICU for the unforeseeable future, I didn't want to burn up anymore of my maternity time than necessary; otherwise, he'd be discharged, and I'd have no time left to spend with him at home. So back to work I went, and thankfully, I was blessed to be working for an incredible company at the time with an even more incredible leadership team. They allowed me a more flexible schedule, so I could be in the office but also spend time at the hospital as needed. And thankfully, most of my work was computer based, so I was able to do it from anywhere as long as I had my computer, Wi-Fi and a cell phone.

I remember my very first day going back into the office I was nervous and anxious, not about doing my job—as I had been in my position for quite some time and, despite being out for the past two weeks, was still highly capable of performing my job—but rather about facing other people, people outside of the small group that I had isolated myself to over the past few weeks. With "my people," I could be vulnerable and honestly lose my shit and not bat an eye. But work was a different story. I needed to be composed, to hold myself together, to focus, and honestly, I wasn't sure I could do that. I worked on the third floor of a building and usually rode an elevator up, but upon arrival that day, I opted to take the stairs, again hoping to sneak in and get to my desk. I just wanted to go to work, do my job and leave and not see anyone.

Like every place I returned to post delivering Beckett, my mind would remind me: "Oh, last time you were here, you were still pregnant." It was a haunting and heartbreaking reminder of everything my world had become. I made it through that first day back in the office but I remember making a big effort not to go into detail about Beckett's condition and all that had transpired when coworkers would inquire. I wasn't ready to talk about it, at least not yet and not to people who were outside of "my people."

As the days slowly ticked by between work and hospital visits, I longed for just one thing, well one realistic thing anyway. I desperately wanted to hold Beckett, to do kangaroo care or skin to skin as they called it. Since the day he was born until now, I was only able to touch Beckett through the holes in the incubator. He was too small, too fragile, too sick to be held. I had asked before, but each time he wasn't medically stable enough. Now and again, he would have good days, and I remember asking the nurse one evening if she thought I could hold Beckett at some point soon. She advised as long as Beckett was stable the next day, I should be able to. She was scheduled to be Beckett's nurse again the following day and said she would be here and would make sure it happened, assuming of course he was up for it. Just like that a tiny glimmer of hope grew inside of my chest. However, I was all too familiar that a change in Beckett's condition could make it impossible, so I didn't let that glimmer of hope shine too brightly.

The next day, I arrived at the hospital knowing from the night nurse and morning update from the neonatologist that Beckett had had a good night and was relatively stable. I asked the nurse from the day before—Alisha was her name—if she still thought I would be able to hold Beckett, and she said I could after we completed his cares at 5:30 p.m. I was excited and scared out of my mind at the same time. The clock seemed to tick ever so slowly until it was finally time. I sat in a recliner chair next to Beckett's incubator and untied my wrap sweatshirt exposing just my nursing tank underneath. It took the careful maneuvers of both Alisha and another NICU nurse to lift Beckett from his incubator and place him on my chest. He was like a tiny rag doll with a million cords, lines and tubes that all had to be carefully readjusted and placed in just the right position. Beckett fit perfectly between my breast, and we tucked his legs and little bottom into my nursing tank to help support him.

Once we were settled, the nurses went about attending to their other tiny patients, and we were left alone, just Beckett and me. All the nerves before holding him, all the compiled worries from the past three weeks began to slowly melt away. Finally, I was able to hold my first born. Something so simple, something so natural, something so many take for granted, but not me. I had bonded with this tiny being for twenty-six weeks and two days while he grew inside my belly before we were separated in the worst of ways. And it had been nineteen days of little more than hand contact, but not anymore. We were together again. His heart against my heart, his tiny head nestled against my chest—to this day I can remember the feeling. It's one of the best feelings in the world, and it's one I will never take for granted.

The days crawled past like flowing molasses in wintertime. Beckett remained relatively stable, which allowed both Ryan and I to take turns holding him when we came to the hospital for visits. However, stable isn't progress, and we needed Beckett to start working towards breathing on his own, eating on his own and maintaining his own body temperature, all things that would be required before we could even begin to think about busting out of the NICU at Saint Luke's. I started to learn, as one does once they become familiar with new places and situations, things that I liked and didn't like about the NICU. For one, I was so thankful that we had a private room at least for the time being. There was one more spot for another baby in Beckett's room, but so far it had remained unoccupied. I also had started to make a mental list of nurses and doctors that I liked and didn't like. People can be qualified for and accomplish the same results in the job they do; however, there are some who just do it better. And at four weeks into our NICU stay, I knew the good ones from the bad. We made sure to ask the good ones to try to keep Beckett as a primary patient, which basically meant that anytime they worked, they should be given Beckett as one of their patients. This created a consistency of care for Beckett, but honestly, for me it gave me peace of mind that Beckett was in good hands, even when I wasn't there.

One of my favorites, whom I've referenced above and will continue to do so throughout Beckett's story, was Alisha. She was there the first day that I was able to hold Beckett, and not only was she extra kind and compassionate towards Beckett, fussing over his position in bed and the way his cords and lines were positioned, making sure to check any sounding alarms with urgency and that his cares and meals were delivered on time, but also towards me. She took time to answer my questions, shared her knowledge of the care plan and brought me tissues when the tears came. But more than that, she put extra effort into the little things in the NICU. When Beckett was twenty-six days old, he finally was able to wear his first outfit. Now with many NICUs, you can bring your own clothes into the hospital, but you run the risk of them being lost in the laundry. And in my case, I didn't even have any preemie clothes—hell Beckett's nursery furniture hadn't even been delivered yet! Anyway, sometimes these clothes had been in the NICU for years and were old and worn, same with the bedding. Alisha always made sure when she was on shift with Beckett that he had cute outfits and bedding. Something that sounds irrelevant and unimportant in the big picture, but one of the fun things that parents look forward to when welcoming a new baby is new clothing and a picturesque nursery to come home to. Sure, ours ended up being nothing like what we anticipated, but Alisha helped ease that sting just a little with her extra efforts.

Beckett's first month of life wasn't celebrated with a photo op focused on a large "one month" sticker stuck on his onesie, as seems to be the tradition in this day and age. Instead, we focused on how far we had come since January 2: from weighing a mere 2 lbs 2 oz at birth, to dropping as low as 800 grams at one point, to the 3 lbs 7 oz he was that day; from CPAP to traditional vent to high frequency ventilator and back again; from 100 percent oxygen support to 37 percent oxygen support; from 2 ml of milk in a feeding to 30 ml; the passing of brain scans. We celebrated how far he had come and reflected on how our days had passed, as well. We had suffered heartbreak watching his struggles and worry in waiting for test results. We had cried tears of sadness and defeat and tears of joy and success. Best of all, we experienced absolute bliss in holding Beckett for the first time, being able to kiss his tiny head and looking into his once fused, shut eyes. We made sure to celebrate every milestone, no matter how minute or ordinary. I read a quote right around Beckett's one-month birthday that said, "If you want to know the value of one month's time, ask the mother of a baby born prematurely." A greater truth has never been spoken.

The second month

Time—that's what premature babies need most. They need time to rest and nutrition to make them stronger, so their little bodies can have enough strength to grow and function as they should. And while I longed with all my being for time to pass quickly so we could get past all these hurdles, it didn't. I can remember sitting in my bedroom pumping, staring out the window and thinking, by the time the cattails in the backyard turn from brown to green, Beckett will be near his due date and hopefully healthy enough to come home. I wished time forward, each day and every day after Beckett's arrival. For each day that passed was another day to heal, another day to get stronger. I dreamed of our discharge day from Saint Luke's, the joyous departure, the hugs from nurses and waves from doctors as we embarked on our next journey at home with a healthy baby.

But on February 5, those dreams of inching closer to the exit doors were blocked by another hurdle. It was a Saturday, and Ryan and I were spending the morning painting our rental property that had been vacated and needed fixing up before it could be rented out again—a sharp reminder that everything else in life doesn't stop when something unthinkable happens. It was midmorning, and I assumed that the call from the hospital was just an update from the doctor or nurse for the day, which was pretty common. We did receive an update, but also learned that little Beckett's heart was broken, literally. Over the past week or so, doctors and nurses had been hearing a murmur, and that day another echocardiogram was performed to paint a better picture of what they were hearing. The echo showed that Beckett's PDA had not only reopened, but was larger than it was to begin with. In addition, the two large chambers of Beckett's heart were showing enlargement. The doctor shared with us that at this time they felt it was necessary for Beckett to have surgery to close up the open valve, which should in turn help with the respiratory issues and enlargement of the two large chambers of the heart that they saw on the echocardiogram.

Once more the optimism and accomplishments of how far we had come seemed irrelevant. The world crashed down around me as I hung up the phone, sliding down the wall I had been leaning on and into a pile of mush among paint brushes and plastic paint liners. Ryan came and gathered me, like he always does when I fall apart, and spoke logic and truth into the situation. If emotions were defined by color, my personality type would lead me to be the most vibrant rainbow you've ever seen, whereas Ryan is able to see life and its obstacles in a very black and white manner. We talked through it, speaking of fears and hopes, frustrations and next steps. In the end, I still hated the idea, but we both knew it was what Beckett needed to move forward. And so, on February 8th, 2011, tiny Beckett had heart surgery.

The morning of surgery, Ryan and I arrived at the hospital around 6:30 a.m. We wanted to spend some time with Beckett before the procedure. The surgery itself was performed in Beckett's hospital room by a specialized cardiologist and neonatal surgical team. We met the cardiologist and anesthesiologist to talk through the procedure and signed all the necessary paperwork. Beckett wouldn't be having an open-heart surgery, but rather an incision would be made around Beckett's left armpit/back area. The incision would be approximately 1.5 inches and would be closed using glue and internal sutures. They would deflate Beckett's left lung to get to the heart and then place a metal clamp on the open PDA vessel on the heart. Once completed, they would re-inflate the left lung and hopefully be done. In addition, we were told all the potential risks and complications that could arise, but when you're at these kinds of crossroads, you just try to understand them and pray like hell they don't happen.

It was then time to leave. I had held it together until that point, and then the tears flooded my eyes and streamed down my cheeks faster than raindrops on the windshield of a speed train. I just wanted to hold Beckett and fix him, protect him. I wanted to trade places with him. I wanted anything but to think about them cutting open my tiny first born. Thankfully, Alisha took an extra shift that week so she could be Beckett's nurse the day of surgery. She met Ryan and I with a box of tissues and assured us Beckett would be okay. She would be right there with him.

The actual procedure only took about thirty minutes, but with all the preparations and post-operation cares, it was quite some time before the cardiologist met with Ryan and I after the surgery. He advised that the surgery went well, and Beckett's PDA was quite large. In fact, it was large enough it required him using two clamps to close it and he advised that without a doubt it was one that wouldn't have ever closed up on its own. Not that you ever want the condition to be worse, but I did feel some validation in knowing we made the right decision for Beckett to have the surgery.

As we started the road to recovery, we waited for the worse as many of the nurses and doctors had warned us that, sometimes after a surgery, preemies will get sicker before they start to show signs of improvement. So, we held our breaths and braced ourselves. Amazingly though, Beckett didn't get sicker. His level of respiratory support did not increase, and we welcomed the uneventful days of "watchful neglect" as we let Beckett rest and recover from surgery.

While he recovered, I wasn't able to hold Beckett, but spent many days reading him books or singing to him softly from outside his incubator. While I was so thankful the surgery had been successful and, thus far, he had not experienced any setbacks, my heart still sank at the sight of his incision. When I looked at the line on his back, the skin sealed together with surgical glue, I saw damage and imperfection. Because, despite all the obstacles he had overcome and all the ones unknown that lay ahead, I had visions in my head of him in three years when we would look back on these early days and remember how absolutely miserable it was but would then look at Beckett and see how perfect he ended up. But now, that line would ultimately be a permanent scar that would forever remind us of these dark and painful days and how our original dreams of a healthy baby were instead replaced with the reality of those with a sick and once broken child.

But as they say, time does heal, and Beckett did recover from his surgery. And while I still wrestled with his scar that seemed to haunt me, we started again on our road towards health with the hopes that a properly functioning heart would help us move ahead with greater force than before. Seven days post surgery, Beckett's respiratory function was tending in the right direction. He was still on the traditional vent, but was only receiving thirty-five assisted breaths per minute. The doctors said that once he got down to thirty to twenty-five breaths per minute and tolerated that well, we could work on switching him over to CPAP, which would mean we could remove the breathing tube and just use a nasal apparatus to assist Beckett with breathing. A major step in the right direction and a glimmer of hope that maybe things would start moving forward with more than one step forward and two steps back, as it felt our entire NICU stay had been thus far.

After making it to thirty-five assisted breaths per minute, Beckett's carbon dioxide levels in his blood started to rise, and the doctors ordered him back up to forty breaths per minute. The nurses also noticed that Beckett was having more secretions than usual in his breathing tube despite being recently extubated and reintubated with the hopes that a new clean tub might help him remain more stable on the thirty-five breaths and continue to advance with weaning off the vent. Due to the increased secretions, cultures from Beckett's breathing tube were tested, and the results showed that Beckett now had an infection in his lungs. Not terribly uncommon as bacteria will find its way into breathing tubes, especially those in place for a long period of time like Beckett's, but for us, another setback.

Once the seven-day course of antibiotics were through, we found we were once again stuck and not making any progress with being able to wean off the vent. Beckett remained at thirty-three breaths per minute and was on 50 to 55 percent oxygen. He was gaining quite a bit of weight, but it wasn't muscle and bone weight; it was all fluid, and my poor baby was so puffy he looked miserably uncomfortable. His skin seemed stretched too tight, and he had rolls and extra chins that shouldn't be present on a tiny preemie. So, another dose of Lasix was ordered, and since his red blood cell count was low, another blood transfusion transpired (transfusion #8). At one point during this time of no progress, Beckett self-extubated himself. He was getting big enough and strong enough that if his hand got a hold of the breathing tube, he could pull it out himself. This happened one day while Ryan and I weren't at the hospital yet and the nurse was hoping she could just put him on CPAP and he would be able to handle it. However, he wasn't responding well and had so many secretions even with the breathing tube out that they ended up needing to reintubate him almost immediately. Not a good sign and perhaps an omen of things to come.

One night, as Ryan and I made our way down the long hallway to exit the NICU, we talked of how we felt frustrated and disappointed. We had hoped that fixing Beckett's heart would help us finally make some progress forward with weaning him off the vent, and his amazing heart surgery recovery with no setback made us believe even more that we were headed in the right direction, and yet we found ourselves once again stuck. Sure, it was great Beckett was stable and many things were working in our favor, but it was so hard not to see the progression towards the next milestone you know you need to meet. In my mind, I knew this was all part of the ride, and while this stage was more like the flat part of the ride, it was annoying. I found I had to take a step back and remind myself Beckett's body wasn't supposed to be doing any of these things yet. He was still supposed to have seven more weeks to grow and develop in my belly before entering this world and being self-sufficient. And so, I needed to practice patience, and Beckett needed more time. All the extra secretions that seemed to be our new enemy were just a result of the excess fluid his body was retaining, and his body was only retaining them because his poor little liver and kidneys were immature. *Time, Natalia, time is all he needs. Be patient.*

Over the course of these weeks, I finally felt like I was starting to come to grips with the life-altering changes Beckett had brought to our lives by arriving fourteen weeks early. In the beginning everything was so hard, and it really truly was. As if postpartum hormones weren't enough, add in pumping, lack of sleep, stress, anxiety, fear, anger and working, and I was a walking basket case encased in a heavy fog. At one point, my primary care doctor suggested and prescribed me antidepression medication. I have no issues with taking these meds, but for me, it was my wake-up moment. I've always considered myself a mentally and physically strong person, and I could see that I was at my own personal crossroads in Beckett's journey. I could continue to dwell and cry, to be angry at all the healthy babies and pregnant moms, to keep people out and not let them in. I could take the antidepression medication and I'm sure it would have helped, or I could mentally change my attitude and my actions to help save myself. And save myself was what I knew I needed to do. Was it easy? Nope. Did I still have bad days? Absolutely. But I learned to compartmentalize life and the issues it threw my way. I focused on the positives each day, what I needed to get done for that day and how I could be the best mama for Beckett. Slowly the fog lifted, and I started to let more people in. I found the more and more I shared Beckett's story with others, the more it became real to me and more accepted by me. I was becoming stronger, and while I was still completely and utterly exhausted, I was able to do more than just barely survive. I was starting to live again.

By the end of Beckett's second month of life, we were still stuck and having issues making any major advancements with weaning off the ventilator. However, Beckett did achieve one big milestone, and that was moving out of the incubator that had been his home since birth. This meant that Beckett was finally able to keep his body temperature high enough without the assistance of the incubator. And true to NICU style, we celebrated this milestone, the moment of joy and achievement and then focused again on the road ahead knowing well more hurdles were likely to greet us along the way.

THE TRANSFER

As the calendar rolled to March, my hopes of being home by Beckett's original due date, which was April 8th, 2011, turned from "definitely possible" to "maybe possible." We had a sixty-day meeting with Beckett's entire care team, which included doctors, nurses, therapists, social workers, etc. It was the first time in two months that I felt like we were talking about weeks ahead instead of just trying to survive the next day or hour. We were able to talk through what needed to happen next—breathing independently, eating via bottle/nursing and not feeding tube, etc.—and ask any questions we had. We talked about support once we were discharged, the developmental screenings Beckett would be seen in clinic for, and so on. It was insightful and gave Ryan and I an idea of what goals we needed Beckett to accomplish and the steps that would lead us there. But like all NICU plans, they never go as intended.

One evening in early March shortly after our sixty-day meeting, Ryan and I headed to the hospital and were excited to see that one of our favorite nurses, Tracy, who had taken care of Beckett the first few days after birth, would have him for the night. We also learned when the night physician rounded that they wanted to give Beckett a CPAP trial around 8:30 p.m. that night. Both Ryan and I were ecstatic. CPAP was essentially respiratory support using just an exterior nasal device that assisted with breathing versus having a breathing tube down the windpipe. It was the next step forward we needed Beckett to take in order to get him breathing on his own. Around 8:15 p.m., we performed Beckett's cares and I remember my excitement for his trial turning to worry. I prayed feverishly in my mind as I completed Beckett's cares, prayers for him to not only be able to function on CPAP, but also for his safety. I was sick to my stomach, and part of me wanted to walk out and come back once I knew whether he would make it on CPAP or not, but I knew I needed to be there for Beckett.

After cares were completed, the doctor, respiratory therapist and nurse extubated Beckett and placed him on CPAP. I felt like I was holding my breath as we waited to see what was going to happen. I was relieved that Beckett didn't give up immediately as he had previously when he was extubated. He was breathing on his own, but he hated CPAP. Luckily, the doctors and nurses had warned us that, in general, babies hate CPAP and this was especially true for babies who were on the ventilator as long as Beckett had been. So Ryan and I basically held Beckett's arms and legs down, in an effort to keep him from pulling the CPAP off his face, and tried to calm him. If he was going to struggle to breathe from his respiratory condition alone, being so worked up was definitely not helping matters.

Ryan and I spoke softly and tried singing to Beckett. We cradled him with our hands. We tried anything and everything to calm him. For the first time ever, I heard Beckett cry. Although he sounded extremely raspy from being intubated for so long, it was still such a sensory overload to me. After about thirty minutes on CPAP, Beckett's oxygen saturations levels began to drop, and his alarm started ringing. Tracy started increasing his oxygen levels each time the alarm sounded, going from about 55 percent to 80 percent. She also discovered listening to his airway and lungs during this time that Beckett had a condition called stridor. Stridor is basically inflammation of the windpipe that makes breathing more difficult as the windpipe is narrower than it should be because of inflammation. The respiratory therapists came and administered a dose of a medication called racemic epi via a nebulizer. Its intent was to reduce the inflammation and make it easier for Beckett to breathe.

The care team really wanted Beckett to calm down so they could get an accurate blood gas reading on him. Again, a blood gas report would tell the care team how well Beckett's body was processing the air he breathed into his lungs and if it was traveling appropriately to his body. They thought that maybe if I were to hold Beckett skin to skin that would help him to calm down and they could get a better reading. I sat in the chair next to Beckett's bed as they transferred Beckett to my chest. Mind you, he was still pissed as can be, and even though he only weighed about 5.5 lbs, he was still thrashing and kicking everywhere. My heart was racing, but I tried to force slow breaths with the hopes that Beckett would follow my lead.

After only about thirty seconds on my chest, I started to notice that Beckett's coloring, which was red from him being so mad, was starting to turn blue and I knew things were headed in the wrong direction. Tracy immediately transferred Beckett back to his bed and called for the doctor and another nurse just as Beckett coded. All of a sudden, time stood still. I stood a few feet away from Beckett's crib and watched as Tracy hit the code button on Beckett's wall and grabbed supplies nearby to start "bagging" him, which basically meant she was performing CPR to try to get Beckett to breathe again. Beckett lay lifeless on his bed. His monitors blinked, his stats crashed and alarms sounded. More and more people came rushing into Beckett's room, all working frantically to bring Beckett back. I couldn't move. I wanted to run to Beckett and plead with him to start breathing again, but I felt as if my own breath was taken from me. I turned to Ryan who was standing by my side and hid my face in his chest. I don't remember having any thoughts in those moments; my mind was numb. After what seemed like an eternity, we started to hear the steady beat of Beckett's heart once again on the monitor. My breath returned to my lungs, and everything in Beckett's room started to move in normal time and with normal sound levels again. Ryan and I stepped out to the NICU waiting room, while the team reintubated Beckett and got him more stable.

It took a day or so before I was mentally able to reflect on the CPAP trial. Beckett had lasted about an hour on CPAP before coding. The entire experience was terrifying, and to this day, I have a hard time thinking about it and discussing it. I've locked it deep inside one of my mental compartments that's stickered with lots of warning labels, and when it does creep into my conscience, my mind quickly tries to replace it with another thought.

After a day or so, I thought back to the trial trying to find the positives: another coping mechanism that the NICU teaches you, even in the most dire situations, find the good. And the positive we walked away with was hope. Beckett had not totally given up on trying to breathe on his own as he had when previously extubated. This time he did try; he just had such terrible stridor that he struggled to breathe easily. So now we just needed to fix his stridor. He was big enough and strong enough to do it; we just needed to make it easier for him to do it. And so that very same night, they started Beckett on a medication called dexamethasone, a steroid. All along our NICU journey, we had been against using steroids on Beckett and reserved them as an absolutely last resort. We had heard about the medication's terrible side effects and potential long-term health risks on tiny babies like Beckett. But that night, we prayed in its favor. It has been such a long, slow, and painful journey, and so we prayed the steroids would be what worked. We prayed that only its positive effects would work in Beckett's body and the negative ones would stay at bay.

The dexamethasone was ordered to be given to Beckett for six days, at which point they would start to ween him down until he was eventually off the medication. A couple days after starting the medication, the doctors again wanted Beckett to complete a CPAP trial. While I was beside myself with worry, I knew it was the next step and that we needed to try again. And so, I prayed that the steroid had worked some kind of magic in Beckett's airway and his stridor would be less severe or even better, totally fixed.

On CPAP trial #2, Beckett lasted about thirty minutes before being reintubated. He started out pretty good, but the doctors who were listening to him about every five minutes could hear the stridor in his windpipe getting tighter and tighter, meaning less and less air was getting through. Even though it technically was another failure, I was relieved when the doctors made the call to reintubate Beckett. It was like we threw him a rescue line before the mother wave swept him under and away again. Once reintubated, Ryan and I spoke with the doctor about what his failure meant. The doctor was in favor of letting the steroid treatment run for two more days and then trying CPAP again. "Then what?" I asked. What if he failed a third time? The doctor advised that he would order a bronchoscopy of Beckett's airway. A bronchoscopy is when a tiny camera is passed down the throat and into the windpipe allowing doctors to see the state of the windpipe. He advised that, when he reintubated Beckett this time, he didn't see the redness and inflammation he expected he would for the strong case of stridor Beckett was presenting. He further stated that it was possible that something was blocking Beckett's airway, something other than just the inflammation. It could be a mass or extra fold of tissue—there would be no way to tell for sure without a bronchoscopy.

I saw no point in waiting two more days. "What if we did a bronchoscopy now?" I asked. "Maybe all it will show us is the inflammation we are already treating and then we will know that Beckett needs more time on the dexamethasone and that's fine. Alternatively, we can wait two more days, have him fail again and then order the bronchoscopy—who knows how long that will take to schedule—and what if it shows us a mass that we can then remove? Why don't we just check for any masses or abnormalities now?" I saw no point in waiting and pressed the doctor to order the bronchoscopy now.

Up until this point, I had felt at the mercy of God's will for Beckett and relied heavily on the knowledge and expertise of the nurses and doctors, trusting they always knew best. But after sixty-five days in the NICU, I was starting to see situations in which I didn't agree with the doctor's plan of care. My father, who is a nurse by education, spoke to me about being an advocate for Beckett. In the beginning, I had no idea what that meant. How could I be an advocate when I knew nothing about caring for a premature infant? But in a little over two months, while I still had no nursing or medical doctor degree, I found situations when I thought doing things different made more sense.

The doctor agreed with my request to do the bronchoscopy sooner rather than later, and at 4:15 p.m. that afternoon, Beckett went to the operating room for his bronchoscopy. While we waited for the time of his scope, we started researching and educate ourselves on what the potential findings could be. We Googled the following terms and tried to wrap our minds around what they would mean for Beckett and what the next steps might be.

Laryngomalacia: Parts of the larynx are floppy, and they collapse causing partial airway obstruction. Most children will usually outgrow this condition by the time they are eighteen months old. This is the most common congenital cause of stridor. Very rarely children may require surgery to repair the larynx.

Subglottic stenosis: The larynx may become too narrow below the vocal cords. Children with subglottic stenosis are usually not diagnosed at birth, but more a few months after, particularly if the child's airway becomes stressed by a cold or other virus. The child may eventually outgrow the problem without intervention. Most children will need a surgical procedure if the obstruction is severe. This problem is most common in premature infants.

Subglottic hemangioma: It is a type of mass that consists mostly of blood vessels. Subglottic hemangioma grows quickly in the child's first few months of life. The child will usually show signs around the age of three to six months. Some children may outgrow this problem, as the hemangioma will begin to get smaller after the first year of life. Most children will need surgery if the obstruction is severe. This condition is very rare.

Vascular rings: The trachea or windpipe may be compressed by another structure (an artery or a vein) around the outside. Surgery may be required to alleviate this condition.

It's funny how when you're facing some kind of medical diagnosis, you educate yourself as much as possible, and then in your mind you always rank the potential outcomes from best to worse. Ryan and I found ourselves doing this over and over again with Beckett's diagnoses. It's never fun, like picking the best of the worse choices ever. From speaking with the care team, we did understand that, if surgery was required to correct any issue that might be found, Beckett would need to be transferred to Children's Mercy Hospital in Kansas City where they had specialized care teams for such procedures. The thought overwhelmed me. For one, the thought of another surgery for Beckett was cause for stress, and then add in the fact that we would be in an entirely new facility where we knew none of the care staff sounded even more stressful. It seems odd to say, but we had actually become quite comfortable in the NICU at Saint Luke's. We knew the receptionists, the doctors, the good nurses. We could easily navigate the iridescent lit hallways that led from the parking garage to the locked NICU doors. It wasn't where we would choose to be, but we had adjusted to being there.

Before the procedure, the anesthesia resident came to review Beckett's chart and ask about his medical history. I found myself getting so upset with his questions as they were forcing me to go back and relive the last two months of Beckett's short life and all the challenges we had already faced. "Beckett was born on 1/2/2011?" "Yes." "And he was born at twenty-six-weeks and two-days gestation?" "Yes." "Looks like he has had quite a few blood transfusions already." "Yes." "And he had PDA surgery on February 8th, 2011?" "Yes." It was exhausting, just like everything in the NICU, so mentally exhausting.

Prior to Beckett being taken to the OR for his bronchoscopy, I was able to hold him, and it was one of the very rare peaceful moments for me while in the NICU. He was sleeping soundly, and we were alone in his room. The alarms were all silent, and the sliding doors that separated Beckett's room from the main section of the NICU were shut, distancing us from the reality that Beckett was a tiny critically ill baby. I gazed at his precious face, which was always plagued with tubes, wires and devices to help hold all those life-saving devices he needed in place. I prayed that the scope would help us discover what was next. I prayed for his safety. I prayed that soon I would be able to see his beautiful little face clear from all these devices.

Beckett's bronchoscopy went smoothly from a procedural stand-point and came back with favorable but frustrating results. The ENT doctor who performed the bronchoscopy advised that Beckett's airway showed no masses or other issues that would require surgery. Instead, he advised that Beckett's vocal cords were just extremely swollen. So, good, no trans-fer would be necessary, but frustrating because time was likely what was needed, more time.

About a week after Beckett's bronchoscopy and his initial dose of the steroids, another round of steroids was ordered when he failed to make any further respiratory advances. We cringed. Again, we did not want to have to use steroids, but we did see good results in Beckett's respiratory function after the first round, and so we held our breath and forged ahead. We knew we were nearing the end of the road in terms of options to help Beckett get over this hurdle. But just as soon as we were preparing for the second round of steroids, Beckett started to have more secretions in his breath-ing tube, and a culture revealed another infection. So the second round of steroids would have to be put on hold while antibiotics were given to treat the infection. After the infection had cleared, the second round of ste-roids would be administered, and sometime thereafter, we would attempt another CPAP trial.

So again, Beckett needed more time. During our time of waiting, Ryan and I quizzed the doctors on all the "what if" scenarios. What if after this next round of steroids he failed CPAP again? He said more than likely they will have to transfer Beckett to Children's Mercy to be seen by a pediatric ENT specialist. From there, they would likely perform additional bronchoscopies, and it was possible that a tracheotomy or surgery would be needed. Again, we prayed, prayed the medication would work, that time would heal Beckett and, by the next CPAP trail, he would soar through. Then he could learn to eat orally. Remember he was being fed by a feeding tube for almost two-and-a-half months at this point, and in the perfect scenario, we would graduate from the NICU, never looking back.

Such wishful thinking, such wishful dreaming . . . time crawled. I've never wished time forward the way I did with Beckett. I was tired of waiting for medication to work, or him to grow, for time to heal. I was growing impatient. I dared to dream of a time when all this would be a distant memory, a time when we would say "Remember when . . ." But I've always been a dreamer, and so dream I did.

On Monday, March 21st, 2011, my cell phone rang sometime after 6:30 a.m. I was still at home and expected the call to be from the attending doctor who was going to advise me of the plan for Beckett that day. It was the doctor, but instead, they were calling to tell me that Beckett had self-extubated himself around 6:30 a.m., and they were placing him on CPAP. I immediately finished getting ready and rushed to the hospital.

When I arrived, Beckett was on 38 percent oxygen (for your reference, room air is 21 percent), but soon that rose to around 60 percent. You could very audibly hear Beckett's stridor as it was quite loud. The respiratory therapist came in and administered the first of what would be four rounds of racemic epi. Beckett was irritable on CPAP, but he would calm down some during the racemic epi treatment. Once the treatment was over and CPAP was back in place, he would get worked up again. The respiratory therapist saw this trend and decided to switch Beckett over to a high-flow nasal cannula. A nasal cannula is basically what you think of when you see someone who is on oxygen: a clear tube running across their face with two small tubes that insert ever so slightly into their nostrils. Beckett was much more tolerable of the nasal cannula than the CPAP.

The attending doctor came to check on Beckett and, given the sound of his struggled breathing and his blood gas report, said he was inclined to reintubate Beckett. My heart sank. I didn't want to give up, not yet. I wasn't ready for a transfer to Children's Mercy. I believed Beckett could do it; he just needed more time to adjust to breathing on his own through his own airway. The doctor wanted to the opinion of a second doctor. So, another neonatologist came and evaluated Beckett, and I could tell she was on the fence about what to do. Thankfully, she turned to me and asked me what I thought we should do. I asked her to give Beckett more time, and she agreed. One hour—that was what we had. One more hour to stay on the nasal Cannula, and they would repeat Beckett's blood gas report. If it trended in the wrong direction, he would be reintubated.

I spent the next hour doing everything to try to keep Beckett calm. His stridor was bad, but it was worse when he was worked up and crying. So, I held, rocked, shushed, patted and soothed Beckett anyway possible. Thankfully, the next blood gas report came back favorable, and so we were granted more time. My entire day on that Monday was living minute by minute, hour by hour, and praying that Beckett would be able to pull through and make it a little bit longer. Treatment after treatment, test after test, he did make it through the day. When he finally settled in for the night around 6:30 p.m., I left the hospital completely drained. The entire day I was on edge. I was focused on Beckett's every move, every breath, every sign of things going downhill or a glimmer of hope he was going to do this. I felt like I had just run for twelve hours straight. My mind was mush, and my body was aching.

Beckett made it through that night on the nasal cannula, but the exam and report from the doctor on Tuesday morning was less than encouraging. While Beckett's oxygen levels stayed static, the morning's X-ray revealed that Beckett's right lung was showing signs of collapse. It wasn't to the point of totally collapsing yet, but some areas were. In an effort to get air moving to those areas of his lung, he was positioned with his right side up and was given vibration treatments to his chest to help stimulate the lungs to open. The racemic epi treatments continued, but the doctor did not write an order to continue the steroids after that day. I think the doctors knew where our ship was headed even though they were holding out hope.

Tuesday I again spent the day trying to console and comfort Beckett. When sleeping, his stridor was nearly silent, but he was not resting peacefully like he used to. He would squirm in my arms and fish for a comfortable position that he could never find. After another full day of being intently present and in tune to Beckett's every move, I left the hospital more exhausted than the day before. I was beside myself. When Beckett was sick early on with chronic lung failure and flipping from one vent to the next or when his heart was broken, he never really looked like he was struggling. Now I had watched for two days straight as his tiny chest heaved to push and pull air into and out of his lungs. I heard him wheezing and coughing trying to breathe. I watched him yawn or sneeze and then start crying, likely because his throat was raw from having a breathing tube down it for more than seventy-five days. It was torture and absolutely heartbreaking. I was not sure how much more I could take or how many more days I could do this. I was tiring, and I knew Beckett was, too.

The sun rose on the morning of Wednesday, March 23rd, 2011, bringing mixed news for Beckett. The bad news was his blood gas reports overnight worsened, so they increased the flow of his oxygen from four to five liters. The good news was the morning X-ray showed improvement in Beckett's lung collapse, and he remained on nasal cannula. Beckett still had stridor and wheezing sounds when breathing, so the attending doctor decided to give Beckett forty-eight more hours of steroid treatments to see if any improvement could be seen. The dose was half the strength of that he had been on in previous treatments, but I was hopeful that it would continue to help any inflammation in Beckett's throat and give him a bit more time to heal.

After spending the last two days of just wanting Beckett to remain on nasal cannula, I wanted to better understand where we should be going from this point. The doctor advised that, ideally, once Beckett completed these additional doses of steroids and was weaned off of them, we would look to see that his stridor and oxygen needs did not increase. Additionally, we would like to start to see better blood gas reports, which would mean we could start weaning Beckett off oxygen assistance. That was the perfect state. At the opposite end of the spectrum, if we continued to see unfavorable blood gas reports or no improvement in Beckett's stridor after the steroids were completed, we were looking at a transfer to Children's Mercy for more specialized airway care. Even though Beckett showed little signs of improvement since Monday morning when he self-extubated himself, I still clung to hope, hope that some miracle would happen and healing would occur.

Thursday came, and I received a call after the morning rounds at the hospital. Beckett was still chugging along though no forward progress could be reported. I needed to be at work that morning but left the office about noon and headed to Saint Luke's. I had an uneasy feeling all morning and was very anxious about getting to the NICU to see Beckett. He was resting in his bouncy chair when I arrived, so I didn't disturb him. Around 2:00 p.m., he started to wake, and so we did his cares and started his food through the feeding pump to try to get him to settle back to sleep. Unfortunately, Beckett was not settling. We tried holding him, placing him on his belly, a bouncy seat, a pacifier, everything, but he was just squirmy and fussy.

The doctor came in to see Beckett, and I was expecting that his orders would be for another blood gas around 5:00 p.m. since Beckett's blood gas earlier in the morning had revealed carbon dioxide in the 70s still. When he came back, he let me know that he thought the best thing for Beckett at this point was to transfer Beckett to Children's Mercy. While I felt that this was the direction that we were headed, it still stung to hear him actually tell me that was the plan, and tears started streaming down my face. Thankfully, the doctor delivering the news was Dr. Anderson, one of my favorites, and was just as compassionate to the parents as the babies he cared for. He gave me a big hug and consoled me, as did Beckett's nurse for the day.

Once settled, I asked about the time frame for the transfer. Dr. Anderson said if Mercy had beds available, he would try to get Beckett transferred that night. After a call, he confirmed that Mercy's transfer team would be at Saint Luke's at 6:30 p.m. to take Beckett. I left Beckett's room and called Ryan who hurried to the hospital. Meanwhile, Beckett was still not settling, and I could tell the staff was on edge at how worked up he was. They made the decision to give Beckett another treatment of racemic epi in an effort to settle him. I'm not sure if it helped or not, but once Ryan arrived, we did our best to try to keep Beckett from crying and getting worked up.

While we waited for the transfer team to arrive, news of Beckett's transfer spread through the NICU, and other staff came to tell us goodbye. It was so hard to say goodbye, as many of these people were ones who had seen Beckett throughout his entire course at Saint Luke's and had taken care of him on his sickest days. Many of them were crying, too. In between those departure visits, I started to pack up the things from Beckett's room. Again, a teary mess doing so. I took down the picture of Ryan and I that hung on Beckett's bulletin board along with his foot prints taken just a few weeks after being born. I thought about erasing "Beckett's Bunk" from his white board on his wall, but I couldn't. I couldn't believe this was happening.

Shortly after 6:30 p.m., the Children's Mercy transfer team arrived in Beckett's NICU room. Of course, as soon as they walked into Beckett's room, my pep talk to try to tell myself to be brave flew out the window. They talked through the transfer process with Ryan and me. Beckett would be taken by ambulance, but no lights and sirens as he was stable. I would be able to ride along with him, but would be in the front of the ambulance. The transfer team did a quick assessment of Beckett, transferred all the monitoring devices to their portable incubator and made a few calls, and we were on our way. As I kissed Ryan goodbye to leave with Beckett, I saw that even his eyes were filling with tears. We had always said we couldn't wait to leave Saint Luke's, but this was not the way we imagined leaving.

The transfer to Children's Mercy went smoothly, and Beckett even feel asleep on the ride. We checked into Children's around 7:30 p.m., and since it was shift change and they were admitting Beckett, we were not able to go back to the bedside with him. I sat in the NICU waiting room and waited for Ryan to arrive. He was not far behind me, and soon one of the front desk staff came and walked Ryan and I through their NICU orientation. Everything was now so different than it was at Saint Luke's. New people, new processes, even the NICU was called the ICN (intensive care nursery) instead of the NICU. After signing some paperwork, the lady settled Ryan and me into the family waiting room to wait until we could go back and see Beckett.

At 9:00 p.m., they still had not called us back to see Beckett, and so Ryan and I went to inquire if we could see him. When we asked the three front desk people, one lady was not compassionate at all and just said, "No, they haven't called yet." I asked, "Well, can I just see where he is?" and she replied, "No, you cannot go back there until they are ready." I was so angry, I was sad, I was exhausted, and this crab of a lady, who lacked all compassion, was not helping at all. Thank God another lady sitting there said, "Stay right here. I will go check and see if the doctor will let you come back." Thankfully, we were able to go back and see Beckett. He was, of course, worked into a hot mess again, but otherwise seemed stable. They did put him back on CPAP, a different one than the one at Saint Luke's, which didn't make him quite as mad. They also had given him a dose of Versed to help calm him.

There was now a huge team of doctors that would see Beckett as Children's Mercy was a teaching hospital, so there were residents, and fellows and attending physicians. There were no private rooms or semi-private rooms in the ICN as there were at Saint Luke's. Instead, there were pods. Beckett was in pod A and was separated from the other tiny patients in the ICN only by curtains, which could be drawn closed. It was sensory overload as we now felt like we had no privacy, medical device alarms were multiplied by five to six times as we could hear other babies' alarms sound nearby and there was always someone coming or going by your spot.

The attending doctor who was overseeing Beckett's care when we arrived at Mercy let us know that Beckett would likely be intubated at some point that evening as his carbon dioxide when he arrived was at eighty-three. They would give him a chance to bring it down, and at his 9:45 p.m. blood gas test, his carbon dioxide had dropped to seventy-eight, which was encouraging. The same doctor also advised us that they were going to try to get the ENT team to see Beckett the next day. Much to our surprise, an ENT doctor was able to come see Beckett that night about 10:30 p.m. He was able to do an upper airway scope bedside. His results were pretty much already known. He said that both of Beckett's vocal cords were moving (we were worried one might be paralyzed from the PDA surgery), but one did look a little stiff. He said that should loosen up over time. He said other than that there was just a ton of swelling.

While we waited for Beckett to calm down after his bedside scope, his nurse let us know that they were able to schedule Beckett to go to the operating room the next day for another bronchoscopy at 1:00 p.m. The doctor had told us when we spoke with her earlier that this would be the plan if they could get Beckett onto the operating room. The doctor also advised that, generally, if they found something while scoping that required surgery, they would most likely operate right then. While I heard what she said, I had nothing left in me to process and react to it. Close to midnight when Beckett was finally settled in, Ryan and I left Children's Mercy. We had to return to Saint Luke's to get my car, and we didn't end up getting home until close to 12:45 a.m. Exhaustion doesn't begin to describe what we were feeling.

At 4:57 a.m. on Friday, March 25th, 2011, my phone rang, and it was the doctor at Children's Mercy letting us know that, at Beckett's last blood gas, his carbon dioxide had risen to ninety, and they were going to reintubate him. Beckett had almost made it four days off the vent, but his body couldn't keep up anymore. Around 6:15 a.m., my phone rang again. It was the doctor letting us know that he was successfully intubated, although it was harder than expected. He was now resting, and his oxygen saturation were in the 90s. I dressed and mentally tried to steady myself for the day ahead.

I managed to navigate my way through the Children's Mercy's parking garage and colorfully decorated lobby and hallways and found my way to the ICN. When I arrived at the hospital, Beckett was resting, but I was so saddened to see the tape around his intubation tube was bloody. The doctor explained the intubation had been very hard, and Beckett fought against it, which caused more irritation of his throat. Nevertheless, I sat at Beckett's bedside still hopeful for a positive day.

Shortly thereafter, the ENT doctor stopped by to talk to me about the bronchoscopy they would do that day and what kinds of things they could find and potential treatment options. What we were hoping to find was some scar tissue that would just be "popped" back open to allow Beckett's airway to be completely clear. But if what they found was extreme swelling, then a tracheotomy might be needed. Again, I tried to think positive and hope for scar tissue or some other small issue that could be easily corrected.

When the staff came to do the rounds, which was now an entire entourage of doctors, fellows, residents and nurses, I was saddened again to learn that Beckett now had kidney stones and gall stones, a side effect of the diuretics that he had been on to help with the fluid retention in his body. There was no treatment for these; they just had to pass. But I knew they are terribly painful, and so Beckett would be suffering through those, in addition to everything else. My eyes welled with tears as I tried to stay strong through the report with the staff. I also learned at this point that the medical team would likely proceed with a tracheotomy that day if deemed necessary based upon how hard Beckett was to intubate. Once they finished with the rounds for Beckett, I immediately called Ryan and shared the news of the potential tracheotomy with the bronchoscopy findings. He rushed to the hospital from work.

Close to 1:30 p.m., we completed the release forms for the scope and anesthesia as well. I kissed Beckett as he was wheeled away to the OR. My heart was ached with pain. Ryan and I were taken to the Ronald McDonald family room, which was located right across from the OR. The doctors would do the scope, fix anything they could and, if a tracheotomy was needed, come talk to us first. About thirty minutes after going to the OR, the entire team of doctors (three ENT pediatric specialists) came and talked to Ryan and me. They said the good news was the lower part of Beckett's airway was completely normal and healthy. The bad news was that the swelling in his upper airways was extreme, and the tissues were so damaged the only way to fix them and let them heal was to get the tube out. And the only way to get the tube out was with a tracheotomy. My heart broke, and silent tears streamed down my face. Ryan and I agreed to the trach, and both sat in silence looking shell-shocked once they left. How could it be that just a few days earlier we felt he was making great progress, and now here we were sitting taking a million steps backwards?

About an hour later, we were able to go back up to the ICN and see Beckett. Of course, upon seeing Beckett, my heart ached even more, and I stood at Beckett's side holding his hand and cradling his head and sobbing for him. Both Ryan and I were absolutely heartbroken. And I was overcome with utter and complete hopelessness. Over the past three months, I tried to stay hopeful and positive. I was strong in fighting along with Beckett. But now I was tired and found nothing left to put my hope in. Everything that we had hoped and prayed would never happen (heart surgery, steroids, trach), had happened. Beckett was the sickest person that I had ever seen in that moment, and I didn't know what the future would hold or how to move forward from where we were.

A NEW NORMAL

Recovery

Beckett received his tracheotomy on a Friday, and we spent most of the weekend by his side. I cannot remember much from those first few days. I think the exhaustion of the week leading up to Beckett's transfer to Children's Mercy Hospital, along with the disappointment of being transferred and the stress of being in a new facility, and the trauma of hearing the news that our baby was sicker than we expected had me in a state of numbness. Once again, I was going through the motions, but not really there.

My one memory is not a fond one. I remember they had secured Beckett's trach with what looked like white shoestrings. They were saturated with blood and discharge from the incision site where his trach now resided. And because Beckett was swollen with excess fluids, the shoestrings looked to be too tight around his tiny neck. It broke my heart then, and thinking of it now, it still does. Why? Why Beckett? Why does he have to suffer so much? It hurt. Everything hurt.

Beckett remained relatively stable the weekend after he received his trach, but did have a spike in temperature and blood pressure, which was usually a sign of infection. In addition, his CBC (complete blood count) test showed an increase in white blood cells, another sign that Beckett had an infection somewhere in his body. Therefore, Beckett was started on two antibiotics, while additional cultures and tests were run to see if they could pinpoint exactly where the infection was and what it was. Beckett's feeds were restarted, still via a NG-Tube (a tube that ran from Beckett's nose, down the back of his throat, to his stomach). The doctors talked about an upper GI (gastrointestinal) scope and giving Beckett a G-Tube, which was essentially a feeding tube that would go from his stomach and exit his body right near his belly button. They asked us about this when he had his trach surgery, but I refused to allow it; I wanted to give Beckett a chance to eat orally first. Beckett was still receiving a number of supplements: sodium, potassium, multivitamins with iron and his diuretic medication. Beckett's ventilator settings were thirty breaths per minute and 27 percent oxygen, which were reasonably low. Beckett also received another blood transfusion (#11) as his blood count was low.

As the calendar turned to April, Beckett continued to heal and recover from surgery. I was at his bedside every day. I was there for the rounds so I could hear the plan of care for that day or week or what goals they were wanting to try to reach. I learned to navigate the hospital and also their new processes and procedures. For example, at Saint Luke's, I could pump bedside, but here they had an actual pump room I went to. I had never felt more like a dairy cow in my life. Think of it as a dressing room, but within each stall was a breast pump, sanitary wipes and milk-collecting containers along with labels and a marker to label your milk with. And if they were all full, I would stand and wait in line, like a bunch of mama cows waiting to go into the barn.

That first week, I watched as trach changes were done to Beckett. The first time was with the ENT doctor who had performed the surgery and the next time with three ICN nurses. Seeing the gaping hole in Beckett's neck leading into his windpipe was terrifying, but not as awful as I thought it would be. I was relieved that the shoestrings were replaced with actual trach neck ties, which were two half-inch-thick felt strings with Velcro on them for attaching to the trach itself and then also behind Beckett's neck to hold the trach in place. The straps were blue in color and decorated with small white stars.

I also participated in and started learning all about tracheotomies and trach care, like the fact that Beckett always had two spare trachs in baggies which were labeled and taped to his hospital bed. In the event his trach came out, we would first grab the same size trach and try to insert it. If we couldn't, we would grab the smaller one and attempt again. It was terrifying to think of doing this in an emergency situation, but it was the new reality our life had become. We learned about trach cares. This essentially meant changing the ties and cleaning the neck, but not removing the trach. This was done every six hours due to Beckett's skin breaking down, causing sores, under where the neck ties would lay on his neck. We learned about suctioning, which meant removing the ventilator tubing from the trach and using a suction machine to clear out any sections that might have accumulated in the trach. So much new, so much to learn. Overwhelmed was again the feeling that plagued Ryan and me.

Beckett began to see a physical and occupational therapist. Mind you, Beckett had been in bed and with a breathing tube down his throat for all of his three months of life. The physical therapist evaluated Beckett's range of motion in his arms and legs as well as his head shape. Beckett had what they call "toaster head" (long and narrow) from laying on both sides of his head too long and stiffness in his arms and legs that they would start to work on with different stretches each day. The occupational therapist also examined Beckett's range of motion, but focused more on his oral stimulation. She looked at his cheeks, tongue, gums and also evaluated his ability to suck. The goal was to let Beckett try to eat orally, and if he couldn't, we would likely have to proceed with the g-tube surgery.

About a week after our transfer to Children's Mercy, all things considered, Beckett was doing quite well. As in previous situations, Ryan and I were amazed by Beckett's strength to overcome and heal. A doctor somewhere along the way told me, "Babies are resilient," and they absolutely are. Any adult going through what Beckett had in his first three months would have had a much longer recovery and with many more setbacks. As for Ryan and me, we were slowly becoming acclimated to the new facility, the new ins and outs of a trach, the next steps for Beckett in his care. And while we dreaded and cursed the tracheotomy at first, we were starting to see the benefits of it already. For the first time ever, we were able to see Beckett's face without all the "hardware" on it. His cheeks were still red from where the medical stickers and tape held his breathing tube for the past nearly three months, but at least now we could kiss his tiny cheeks if we wanted to. We were also able to interact with Beckett so much more. We could now, after some training, get Beckett in and out of his bed on our own to hold him. And the trach would allow Beckett to be much more mobile, so he could start working on his physical strength and head shape. Finally, the trach would allow Beckett to try to eat orally, which could not be done with the breathing tube.

As for me, my heart had been broken (again), and mentally I allowed myself some grace to mourn my dream of Beckett being successfully extubated and a cheerful discharge from Saint Luke's. It had been, as they say, "a long week." I embraced the love and support from family, friends and sometimes complete strangers. One of my weaknesses is I have a hard time asking for and accepting help. But now I needed it. I needed home cooked meals, gift cards for gas as we drove back and forth to the hospital day after day, uplifting text messages and cards. The outpouring of love and support from my tribe and community fulfilled me and gave me strength, strength to not fall into the dark hole I had previously inhibited but to rise again, to be the mother and advocate Beckett needed me to be. So, while I still felt empty inside at times, I forged ahead sustained by kind words and gestures and began to dream new dreams of what our future with Beckett would look like.

Progress

Two weeks post Beckett's transfer and trach surgery, I returned to work. It was difficult to do as I wasn't nearly as comfortable leaving Beckett at Children's as I was at Saint Luke's. A new facility and not knowing the care staff made it hard to not be there every day just to ensure he was given the best care. However, I dreamed of the day he would finally be able to come home and still have some maternity leave time left to enjoy being at home with him. That and the stress and fear of what our next medical bill would be kept me focused on trying to retain my income while balancing all else.

The biggest accomplishment Beckett made post his trach surgery, besides being on much less ventilator support, was seen in our attempt to feed him orally. I left work early one day to ensure I would be there for his feeding trial. Upon arriving, I felt optimistic about the trial. You see, while Beckett was at Saint Luke's, they had performed frequent oral stimulation using breast milk. This essentially meant they would dip a Q-tip in my breast milk and then allow Beckett to taste the milk and move small amounts of it around in his mouth, even sucking on the Q-tip if he wanted or was able to. The idea behind the practice is that the stimulation would help to develop oral feeding skills later down the road and provide something pleasurable in an intubated baby's mouth instead of all the tubes they become accustomed to. At the time, the practice was uncommon and considered somewhat risky with the potential of aspiration, but Beckett always loved it and seemed to process the milk well in his mouth. Thus, I had an optimistic attitude when it came time for the feeding trial.

The occupational therapist (OT), whose name has now left me but whose face I can still see clear as day, placed 20 ml of my breast milk in a bottle and added a thickening agent. Since the ENT team advised that Beckett could have a stiff or paralyzed vocal cord(s), the thicker milk would be easier to swallow and reduce the risk of him aspirating. She started slowly, but Beckett took to the bottle right away. When it was all over, he ended up taking 15 ml of milk orally, which at the time was about 30 percent of his regular feedings. I was *so, so* happy! Beckett had been able to eat orally and had done so without a drop in his heartrate or an increase in need of oxygen support and had mastered the skill of pacing himself (drinking some milk and then pausing to breathe before drinking some more). It was the first good news in what seemed like forever, and it felt good. The OT spoke with the doctor who was going to allow Beckett to eat orally twice in a twenty-four-hour period and then, assuming that everything was going well, would continually increase his feedings to all oral when he was ready.

April 8th, 2011, proved to be an emotional day for me as it was Beckett's original due date. I remember reflecting throughout the day on our journey so far: the ups, the downs, the heartbreak, the scars, Ryan and my relationship, the love from our family and friends. That afternoon as I held Beckett in my arms in one of the leather reclining chairs that we would occasionally have to steal from another pod mate because there were never enough for everyone, I stared at Beckett's face as he slept in my arms. I felt like, *Here we are, the day you were supposed to come into the world, and yet I feel I have already lived a lifetime with you.* So much had happened in the last three months, so many emotions, so many trials, just so much. When the sunset, I was happy to watch the calendar flip to April 9th, 2011, like I had been holding my breath the entire day knowing my original dreams of this day were gone, and now the day was gone, too. I could breathe again, and now I would focus on what lay ahead.

Beckett had become what they called a "Feeder and Grower" baby in the ICN, which for once was a label that we were good with. This essentially meant he was no longer critically ill and just needed to eat and grow for the time being. So, while we waited for Beckett to continue to eat and grow, Ryan and I practiced being trach parents and completed the training we would need for when Beckett would be discharged.

One evening, Ryan and I gave Beckett a bath for the first time. I'm sure he had had baths before, but usually they were done later in the evening when the ICN floor had less activity and the nurses had more time, and by that time, Ryan and I had usually headed home for the night. But on this night, Beckett's nurse brought an infant tub on a rolling cart to his bedside filled with warm water. We undressed Beckett, removing his onesie as well as all his sticky monitors from his body, and maneuvered around his ventilator tubing that was connected to his trach. Anyone who's bathed an infant before knows it's not easy, and Beckett's medical situation added another level of complexity to the entire situation. It was chaotic. Ryan tried to keep Beckett from sliding around in the tub while I washed him, and the nurse helped hold all the tubing that still needed to be connected. Beckett had mixed emotions about it all: one moment calm, and another making a crying face. Remember that, even though the breathing tube was out, the trach didn't allow any air to flow through Beckett's vocal cords, and thus he still made no sounds. You could only tell he was crying or upset by looking at his facial expression. I had brought my video camera to document such a milestone, but we would have needed a fourth person to run the camera since we all had our hands full!

As the days passed, we continued to practice feeding Beckett his bottles and participating in trach cares. We began to understand from the rounds with the ENT team that Beckett would be allowed to come home with a trach and still on the ventilator. However, he needed to be at a specific level of support and stable for that to occur. In addition, he needed to be cleared in any other areas that were a concern as well.

On April 15th, 2011, Beckett had an OPM, or a swallow study. They wanted to validate using additional tools that Beckett wasn't silently aspirating before they would allow him to take all feeds orally and allow us to switch from the hospital-grade ventilator over to the version of a home ventilator that we would eventually go home with. I was present for the study that was conducted in the X-ray department. The staff added barium to Beckett's milk, and the OT had thickened multiple bottles to different thicknesses ranging from "thin" (no added thickener, just regular breast milk) to "nectar," to "syrup," to "honey," each one getting progressively thicker as implied from the names. I watched as the OT fed Beckett the different thicknesses of milk and the radiologist and OT discussed what they were seeing either on the screen or from Beckett's monitor. When it was all said and done, they were able to confirm he was not aspirating on the nectar consistency and decided he handled it the best and thus they would stay with that level of thickness for the time being. With that change, they started to allow Beckett to take all his feeds via a bottle and also switched him the next day to the home-grade ventilator. The home-grade ventilator had all the same settings as the hospital-grade ventilator; however, it could not offer the same support and thus there was some concern, that the change might impact Beckett. Beckett seemed to love all the milk and could have cared less about the ventilator change. We also completed our trach CPR class at the hospital, something we hoped to never have to use, but absolutely vital we knew if the situation arose.

On Sunday, April 24th, 2011, we celebrated our first holiday with Beckett: Easter. There were no baskets or person dressed up as the Easter Bunny to visit. In fact, it really didn't feel like Easter at all. It was just another day in the hospital and one that reaffirmed my determination to get the heck out of the hospital before the next holiday rolled around on the calendar.

Red Tape

The next week passed without any major changes for Beckett. He ate, he passed stool, he remained stable on his home ventilator settings, and so on Monday, April 25th, 2011, I headed to the hospital earlier than normal as I wanted to try to talk to the discharge planner before she left for the day. I was ready to have a date for discharge and get moving towards it. At this point, we had been in the hospital since January 2nd, 2011, 113 days. We were tired of all of it and ready to be home. I was told the previous week that Beckett's home ventilator from the DME company had been ordered. Therefore, I was shocked when the discharge planner advised that it was not there as there was an issue with our insurance. *What? And why am I just now finding out about this?* I felt my face turn red with anger. Up until this point, our insurance seemed great. It was providing for all costs, and we were paying what seemed like a minimum out-of-pocket fees compared to the statements we would receive in the mail, some of which were for six-figure amounts.

What I found out was that our insurance would cover the DME (Durable Medical Equipment) supplies (ventilator, suction machine, trach supplies, oxygen tanks, etc.) with no issues whatsoever. The issue arose with the in-home nursing care. You see the Children's Mercy home ventilator team required twenty-four-hour in-home nurses be provided if a baby is going home with a trach and on a ventilator. An understandable requirement as someone with a medical background would need to provide round-the-clock care for the baby, a burden that the team didn't feel a family could adequately manage without the help and assistance of a nurse being in the home to help perform care day and night so the parents could work, or sleep, and, in the worst case, provide lifesaving cares if needed. I found out from the discharge planner that our insurance provided $2,000 per person per year in home health services, and that figure wasn't even enough to cover one day of nursing for us. I felt frustrated and discouraged all at once. Here we were after four months of literally fighting for Beckett's life, going through hell and back, and now we were being held at the hospital because of a policy by our insurance company.

I asked the discharge planner what options we had. One was to have Beckett's social worker and the doctor that ran the vent clinic write a letter to petition the insurance company to try to get more in-home nursing dollars, a process that was not guaranteed and of course would likely take anywhere from three to four weeks to get through all the red tape and get the necessary approvals. The other option was to get Beckett off the ventilator, another slow process that would likely take more than four weeks. So, we were left with no other option but to pursue both and sit and wait to see which one might happen first. Frustration doesn't begin to describe the situation.

Finally, on May 4th, 2011, we received notification that our insurance company would provide in-home nursing as long as medically necessary. Praise the Lord! Now it seemed we had all our ducks in a row, and we would be able to start checking off all the other requirements to get Beckett home at last.

Preparing for a Homecoming

I am a distance runner, and anyone who's completed a long and intensive run knows that the last quarter mile of the race nearly kills you. Your arms and legs burn with intensity from being overworked, your heart is beating so fast and so loud you can't hear much else besides it's rhythmic thumping as your lungs gasps for air. Your body seems to start to lock up just as you want to sprint towards the finish line and give yourself a much-needed break. The end of Beckett's time in the hospital felt much the same. There were still so many boxes that had to be checked before we could bring Beckett home. But at this point in our journey, I was nearing a mental breakdown, which gave me the sensation that, although I could see the finish line, I wasn't sure I was going to even make it, let alone cross it.

Every morning I awoke with my stress level already heightened for so many reasons. One was I was utterly exhausted. I continued to wake every three hours at night to pump milk for Beckett. I can remember so many nights my alarm would sound, I would turn on the light, sit up in bed, hook everything up and start the pump, only to fall asleep and be awakened to the sensation of milk overflowing from the bottles I was filling. I was beyond exhausted.

In addition, while we loved some of the caretakers at Children's Mercy and overall received good care, I had major anxiety not being there all day, every day. This was for a couple of reasons. One was there were some nurses and physicians whom I just did not trust with Beckett's care. Sad to say, but after so long in an ICU, you just know the good from the bad.

Another was that, without being there for the daily rounds and being Beckett's advocate, things that needed to be done just did not get done. Daily rounds are done in all ICUs and are in essence a morning discussion by the entire care team, generally bedside of the patient, to discuss the current medical state/condition of the patient and the plan of care for the day. Therefore, if I was absent from rounds, the tests that were needed to go home were not ordered and planned. And because Beckett was stable and relatively healthy when compared to his fellow ICN neighbors, he was often moved down on the to-do list as his condition was not a priority in comparison to his more critical peers. An understandable necessity, but when you've been inpatient for over 125 days, you just want to go home.

Pile on top of all that, I was still trying to be successful in my career, re-rent our townhouse that was adding to our current financial stress of paying two mortgages, organize the details for Beckett's discharge, manage the house and so on. You might be able to see how I was crawling to the finish line, but unsure of if and how I would actually make it there.

Both Ryan and I's families were super supportive during this time, but as a daughter, it was my parents who bore the brunt of the stress vents and worry about Beckett's care, or lack of it. Like all children still seeking the advice and guidance of their parents when charting the unknown, I too would call and vent about a doctor I didn't like and how some test needed to go home wasn't ordered because I had a meeting that I couldn't miss at work. And then I'd ask them, "How am I supposed to do it all?" Mind you, Ryan would help when he could, but his profession required him to travel nearly every week, and so that left me to do most of the day-to-day handling of Beckett's care. Ultimately, in May of 2011, my parents made the decision that my mom would take temporary leave from her job, leaving my dad in Saint Louis and come live with Ryan and me in Kansas City to help me get Beckett home.

And so, each and every day, my mother was there sitting in Pod A of the ICN at Children's Mercy Hospital. She navigated the thirty-minute drive from our home through downtown Kansas City and through the colorful maze of parking garage, and hallways lined with children's art and wagons used to transport sick children from one area to the next. She arrived with her notebook and pen, and if anyone knows my mom knows she's a note taker and maker. She knew the list of items that needed to be completed to get Beckett home and so would listen to the rounds and then advocate for those to be ordered or scheduled and be done so as soon as possible, reporting back to me each day who had been in attendance when rounding, what was ordered, what was outstanding. And like all moms, she helped around the house and ensured I ate a wholesome meal most nights, too.

On Friday, May 6th, 2011, we attended a pre-discharge meeting for Beckett where we learned that they were targeting a tentative discharge date of May 31st, 2011, assuming all tests were passed, equipment/supplies were ready and nursing care was available. And so, we crawled forward some more.

Beckett had a customized stroller that arrived at his bedside one day. It was basically a two-seat stroller with the second seat removed and shelves added to store his ventilator, suction machine and all other medical equipment he needed while in transport. The medical supply company delivered Beckett's home vent to the hospital on a Thursday, but it had to go through some testing before Beckett was finally switched over to it on the following Monday, May 9th, 2011. The medical equipment supplier also came to our home to do an evaluation. They tested all the outlets in Beckett's room, measured doors and counted steps into the house and to Beckett's room. They also advised us that we would be on a "priority list" for electricity and phone service should there ever be an interruption of service, something that had never crossed my mind until that point, but a new worry to add to my ever-growing "what if" list.

Beckett had a final MRI of his head, which came back normal, meaning that all the anatomy of the brain (lobes and lumps) looked how they should for a baby Beckett's size. He passed his car seat test which required him to sit in his car seat for 90-minutes with no episodes. Beckett seemed unfazed by all of it. By this point, he was stable and the care team was making little to no adjustments in the ventilator settings to keep him that way and ultimately get him home. During the daytime, he was up to eight hours on CPAP and the ventilator with a two-hour break and then back on CPAP for another four hours. Beckett was eating every four hours and was taking down 110 to 120 ml of milk, roughly the equivalent of 4 oz at each feeding. His milk at this point was still being fortified and thickened. Medication-wise, he was still on a diuretic, potassium chloride, sodium chloride and a multivitamin with iron. He weighed in at a whopping 9 lbs 12 oz. Likely not even on the grown chart for a typical four-month-old, but he seemed like a giant to us.

Ryan and I also completed lots of training and testing. We had training with the medical equipment supplier on proper use of the home ventilator, suction machine, apnea monitor and pulse oximeter. We learned how to make adjustments to the ventilator settings, troubleshoot potential errors as well as clean and maintain all the equipment. The ventilator was probably the trickiest as there was "Peep," "Pressure Control/Support," "Rate," "Oxygen Level" and about a million combinations between those different adjustment tools. Thankfully, we only needed to know how to make changes, and the home ventilator team who would follow Beckett once discharged would tell us what the settings needed to be.

The final hurrah, if you will, took place in the form of a two-night stay inpatient at Children's Mercy where Ryan and I would essentially have to care for Beckett with minimal assistance from the care staff at the hospital. This would be our last and final test. And so, on Saturday, May 28th, 2011, my Mom returned back home to St. Louis and Ryan and I checked ourselves into Children's Mercy Hospital. Equipped with our own suitcase of clothes and items to stay, we loaded up Beckett from his spot in Pod A and brought him to a private room, equipped with a full-size bed, small table, recliner, refrigerator, TV and small private bathroom with a shower. Just getting Beckett moved there was proof and insight into how much work would be waiting for us at home. Babies have a lot of "baggage" as is. Add in a baby with a trach on a ventilator and an apnea monitor who needs suctioning and oxygen support, and you look like the Beverly Hillbillies coming down the way. It was a lot!

But we were there, and we settled into our room. We spent the next forty-eight hours learning everything we could. We would go for walks around the ICN, mostly because that was all there was to do, but it made us very good at transporting Beckett, learning to unhook and re-hook the lines and how to organize the stroller to make it work best for us. Food-wise, we could order anything we wanted from room service and it would be delivered to our room. Sounds lovely, but if you've ever eaten hospital food, you know you aren't missing much. I can only recount minimal memories from our two-night inpatient stay. One was it was long and boring. With limited things to do, the days seemed to last forever. And two, it was exhausting. No one sleeps in a hospital to begin with, and when you are in a full-size bed with your 6'2" husband and the primary caretaker of your stable, but still compromised infant son who has alarms that beep and lights that flash all night, forget about sleep.

Beckett had no episodes while with us, and there was never a point where we needed the nurse's assistance. Monday, we left the hospital, our bodies needing rest, but our hearts racing with excitement. Next day would be a big one—Beckett was finally coming home.

HOME SWEET HOME

150-days

21-weeks

5-months

That was how long we had waited for this day, Tuesday, May 31st, 2011, the day when we would finally be able to bring our first-born son home. The day when we could put behind us the daily grind of trying to be present at work and the hospital and balance all other things, the day when seeing our son would mean walking into the next room instead of a thirty-minute drive, navigating a parking garage and security check-in, the day when, for the first time in his five months of life, he would feel fresh air and be outside, traveling home and into his cozy room we had waiting for him. This was the day.

My memories of moments from this day are blurred: some are etched picture perfect into my mind, and other moments gone, unable to be recalled in the frenzy of all that was to happen. I remember signing the discharge paperwork, ensuring follow-up appointments were scheduled and that I had the home ventilator team's emergency number stored in my phone. I remember loading Beckett and his stuff from Pod A and saying goodbye to some of the pod mates we had befriended during our time at Children's Mercy.

I remember an entourage of people surrounding us: the current care team and two of our primary nurses from the ICN who had been with us our entire time at Children's; Valerie, who was on shift that day and had been caring for Beckett before our departure; and Jessica, who came into the hospital on her day off just to see us off with well wishes and the gift of a sign language book, something we had talked about during one of her many shifts with Beckett. Then there was the home ventilator team of nurses and doctors, the discharge planner, the medical equipment supplier and our in-home nurse who would ride home with us. It felt like 25-people were there and in hindsight there probably was that many.

We slowly made our way to the front entrance of the hospital where the circle drive allows patients to be dropped off or picked-up. Ryan pulled the car around to load us and all the medical equipment and supplies which would now become a constant for us. We paused taking a few pictures, but besides the somber feeling of knowing we likely wouldn't see our beloved primary nurses again, I felt zero sadness or hesitation in leaving. And so, with Beckett loaded, all his medical equipment stored and accessible in case we needed them during the drive, we said our final goodbye. I crawled into the back seat with Beckett, his in-home nurse rode up from with Ryan and, just like that, we were gone.

As our wheels turned away from the hospital, I caught the most perfect picture of Beckett. He was snuggled in his car seat, the window visible just beyond him. His tiny head was propped into place with two baby blankets rolled up to keep his head from falling to either side. One of his hands was on his chest, and the other was holding his ventilator tubing that was attached to his trach. But what made this picture perfect was his expression—he's smiling. As if to say, "Yeah, Mom and Dad, we did it! We finally made it! Let's go home."

Reflecting back, never did I think when I found out I was pregnant that this would be the road Ryan and I would have to walk down. Never in my plans for our first child did I plan on going into labor at twenty-six weeks and spending the following five months thereafter in the hospital. Never did I plan to have to sign release form after release form for medical procedures and surgeries, or have my heart broken watching our baby be taken away for surgeries or being resuscitated after turning blue after an unsuccessful extubation. Never did I plan to learn about oxygen saturation rates, PDA heart surgeries and tracheostomies or how to operate a ventilator because my baby would need me to. Nothing that I thought or had planned to happen actually happened. But let me tell you what did happen . . .

I realized the miracle of the human body and its ability to grow and nurture a baby. I realized just how precious life is. I know we all say these things, but I felt and witnessed them firsthand. There were days early on when we weren't sure if Beckett's little lungs could hold out. And on those days, I thanked God for each passing minute and the promise of each future minute as a chance for Beckett to grow stronger and get better. There were the minutes and hours after Beckett's heart surgery and trach surgery when I wasn't sure how Beckett would ever recover, but somehow, he did. Babies are miracles, especially resilient premature babies like Beckett. I realized the amazing love and kindness of the human spirit. From the moment Beckett arrived into this world, we received incredible support from family, friends and sometimes complete strangers. Cards, flowers, balloons, kind words, encouraging notes, meals, gifts, gift cards, money, hugs, tears, prayers, reality checks . . . I can think of *so* many days over that five-month period when Beckett was so sick, Ryan and I were exhausted and our tribe supported us, lifted our spirits and gave us the strength to face another day, sometimes a very uncertain day. There is a quote that says, "Be kind, for everyone you meet is fighting a hard battle." This quote still guides me every day in remembering the kindness we were shown by so many during our hard battle. I realized my own strength and faith. No doubt both were tested, usually at the same time and sometimes day after day, after day. Nevertheless, I felt all the trials and tribulations had made me a person of greater strength and stronger faith. So many days I would repeat to myself over and over, "I can do all things through Christ who strengthens me," as I had no idea how I would make it through the day. No doubt God lifted me through those days and watched over Beckett on his sickest days. I realized the healing power in being open and sharing Beckett's story with others. Shortly before Beckett was born, I decided to start an online blog. The original thought was I would update it mostly for friends and family of random happenings with our little family, and it would be an outlet for me to write, something I had always enjoyed. However, after Beckett was born, the blog ended up being a tool to update not only worried family and friends, but also followed by hundreds of thousands of viewers from all around the world. Some of my most unguarded emotions were put into those posts, therapeutic to my own suffering and helpful to others going through difficult times, as well. And lastly, I realized I had an amazing partner who stood by my side. While Ryan was just as blindsided by all of this as I, he never revealed fear or sadness. He was my rock. He held me up on Beckett's sickest days, made me laugh in the aftermath and stood by my side through it all. I've been told that the death or illness of a child can either break apart a couple or bring them closer together. I knew we still had a long road to travel, but I felt like we could make it through anything after the gauntlet we had survived over the last five months.

And so home we would arrive where we would unload everything, settle in for the time being and take a much-needed pause from what our life had become, and instead of "what's the next goal Beckett needs to reach," we let ourselves live in the "let's enjoy the moment" briefly, for we knew that, even though we had summited the mountain and crossed that finish line, Beckett's road to health was far from over.

FINDING OUR WAY

We decided we wanted Beckett to spend the majority of time in our living room. Our home was a one-and-a-half story, which meant the master bedroom was on the main floor and Beckett's room was upstairs. Thus, we wanted Beckett to be closer to our room, but not in our room because that would mean the round-the-clock nurses who would be helping us care for him would also be in our bedroom. Therefore, we had essentially turned our living room into Beckett's nursery. We had a Pack 'n Play, and all his medical supplies were organized in one of those plastic rolling drawers you can buy from Walmart. We had blankets and oxygen tanks and diapers and clothes. Thankfully, our living room was good sized, but it still looked like a combination of a TV room, nursery and hospital room.

The first week with Beckett at home went smoothly. He remained stable on his ventilator settings and seemed to be enjoying the peacefulness of being at home too, as there was not nearly the same amount of noise and lights and interruptions as the ICN. To this day, I claim Beckett is a great sleeper because he learned to sleep in an ICU. If you can sleep there, you can sleep anywhere. He would feed at 9:00 a.m., 1:00 p.m., 5:00 p.m., 9:00 p.m., 1:00 a.m. and 5:00 a.m. His medications were given at 9:00 a.m. and 9:00 p.m. feedings. Trach cares were performed every night usually before bedtime. Baths were given every other night in the living room. We would bring a small baby tub, which had a drainage plug in the bottom of it, in the living room and then haul buckets of water from our master bathroom to the tub. Except for being more work to haul in the water and haul it back out when done the baths usually went smoothly. However, one time we forgot to plug the drain before dumping in a five-gallon bucket of water. I was sure we had ruined the carpet and floor.

Even though we had twenty-four-hour-a-day nursing at our home, I selfishly wanted none of their help. I had been waiting for months to have my baby home, to be able to care for him myself, to snuggle with him alone on the couch, to bond as a family. Now I felt like my every moment was being watched and shared with some stranger whom I didn't even know on my couch. I understood why the home ventilator team required nursing to be in place in order to allow these medically fragile kids in the home setting; the care is exhausting and requires not just know-how, but hypervigilance. But I was confident in my ability and wanted to do it all by myself. Furthermore, as the weeks passed and the characters who filled the couch changed, I quickly lost all confidence in the skill level and professionalism of the nurses who showed up on our doorstep.

We had nurses that would "no show" for their shift without communication, others who showed up reeking of smoke, nurses who would fall asleep at night on our couch or suction Beckett too deep causing him to cough and gag. And so, they became a fixture in our home, but one which only charted everything I was doing. I still got up and did all Beckett's nightly cares and feedings and rarely left them alone to watch Beckett.

On June 16th, 2011, nearly two weeks after discharge, Beckett had his first follow-up appointment at the special care clinic at Children's Mercy. He was tracking well for his growth (11 lbs 5 oz), relatively speaking, of course, and based upon labs, they discontinued his diuretics and reduced his sodium chloride medication. From a ventilator perspective, he was now on CPAP, twenty-four hours a day, which meant the ventilator still provided him with continuous airway pressure, but he wasn't receiving any support that made him take a breath or set numbers of breaths per minute. He was also just on room air, meaning he no longer needed supplemental oxygen from one of the portable oxygen tanks. Ryan and I left the appointment feeling great. Progress forward—that was all we wanted at this point, stability and progress. Driving away Ryan said, "Man, I don't miss that place at all." I couldn't agree more. After 150 days in the hospital, that was the last place we wanted to be.

Shortly after that appointment, our in-home nursing hours went from twenty-four hours a day to twelve hours a day, which was just at night. At the time, this was a welcome change in my book. After all, I was back on maternity leave, and besides being tired as all new moms are, I could care for Beckett independently. And the cut in nursing hours came at a good time, as Beckett started to have many visitors. During Beckett's time inpatient, both our parents were able to visit Beckett, but never hold him or stay too long as we were limited in the number of visitors that could be bedside at one time. So, of course, once home, they wanted to come visit, as well as extended family members and friends who had never been able to meet Beckett.

We were no dummies to the potential dangers and serious consequences that could occur should Beckett catch some kind of illness during his interactions with more people, and thus we had some strict ground rules at our home. Upon entering, everyone was asked to remove their shoes and wash their hands. Obviously, no smoking, but we also asked visitors to limit their use of perfume and cologne if coming to visit. Anyone who felt even the slightest bit sick, we asked to stay away, and no children were allowed to meet Beckett. I was the big bad sheriff when it came to these rules as my biggest fear was catching an illness and ultimately ending up back inpatient at Children's Mercy, going nine hundred steps backwards from the direction we wanted to be going. And just the thought of being inpatient again gave me so much anxiety that I had no problems speaking up to friends and family members about their visit, even if they thought I was being rude or over the top.

As we slowly allowed more family and friends to meet Beckett, one thing that always stung me a bit was how uneasy Beckett's visitors were to be around him. Of course, I didn't expect everyone to be as comfortable as I was around him, given the extra equipment and tubes and wires going everywhere, but it hurt to see people hesitate to want to hold him or gawk at all the equipment. I did my best to help explain his "stuff" to them in the simplest way to make them comfortable, and then I moved on. But it always burned me a little and left me with a new approach and attitude when meeting anyone with any kind of physical abnormality or disability.

As summer rolled on, Beckett continued to thrive at home. He was gaining weight, weaning off the ventilator and making strides developmentally. About monthly, we would make the trip down to Children's Mercy to see the home ventilator team, take new measurements, make new adjustments to his ventilator and be sent on our way home. Developmentally, Beckett had a lot of catching up to do. During his first assessment with Missouri First Steps, a state early intervention program for children until age three with disabilities or developmental delays, Beckett's skills placed him at two months old, but at that time, he was chronologically almost seven months old. Thus began our sometime weekly in-home appointments with an Occupational Therapist (OT), a Physical Therapist (PT) and a Speech Therapist (ST). Somewhere in July, our in-home nurses' hours were cut to zero, which seemed fine at the time. We had planned to hire private in-home care for Beckett when I returned to work mid-August, and besides needing one other person to help me with trach cares each night, the nurses really didn't do much for us, or at least we didn't use them as much as we could have.

In the time leading up to me returning to work, we were like any new parents. We doted over Beckett, giving him all of our attention, spending time on the floor for tummy time or reading books or snuggling on the couch during afternoon naps after dragging over his ventilator and monitors, laughing when he would crack a smile or pass gas at the dinner table while we ate. Ryan was still traveling regularly for work, but when home, he made Beckett's world go around. He could get him laughing with some beep-boxing mouth tricks, and even just a simple "hello" from Ryan would leave Beckett bug-eyed and smiling. Ryan was like most new dads caring for a newborn baby. Beckett would end up with poop everywhere after a diaper change, where he would put the diaper on Beckett backwards. He wasn't the best at consoling Beckett when upset and would from time to time give Beckett dog toys instead of baby toys to play with. But he tried to do his best. We both did, truly, as new parents, a baby like none other and an uncharted path for being or moving forward.

As my time on maternity leave drew to an end in August of 2011, my mom once again came to our saving grace to help us care for Beckett. With the insurance company no longer allotting us any additional nursing hours and finding a suitable caregiver being near impossible, she agreed to stay for a few weeks until we could find someone or maybe even get Beckett closer to at least being off the ventilator. Returning back to work made everything go into warp speed. I loved my job, loved my co-workers, and that made it all worth it, but it was hard, like *really* hard. I was a human resources manager who managed all of our company's domestic and international relocations and assignments. I loved it, but it often meant early morning and late evening calls to meet with teams overseas, off-hour fire drills as someone's personal belongings had gone up in flames in a London warehouse or phone calls pleading with an international school in Dubai to ensure enrollment for one of our expat assignee's children, someone detained at customs trying to cross into a country or, worse, been arrested. Moving is a very personal experience, and thus, I often carried the trials of our nomadic associates as my own, adding to my own personal stress. During this time, I had made the decision to stop pumping breastmilk for Beckett, so that was off my plate. Beckett was a great sleeper, but that didn't mean we didn't have nightly alarms from his ventilator that required me to go check on him and clear them. Ryan's travel schedule ramped up, an unfortunate necessity of his job, but one that left me alone to work, manage

Beckett's care, try to find a nanny of some kind, run our home, manage our rental property, and so on. Yeah, it was hard.

By the time September came, we were all tired. I was able to hire a private nanny/caregiver for Beckett even though it costed us a premium in price, and my mom returned home, giving her a much-needed break. Beckett was now completely off the ventilator, and so at our monthly appointment, I asked about the next steps to getting Beckett's tracheotomy removed and closed up. After all, he was doing great, and we were all ready for the craziness of living life with a trach to be over so we could go back to a normal life. I learned that later that month we would meet with the ENT group at Children's Mercy. During that appointment, they would perform an upper airway scope and allow Beckett to try a Passy Muir value. It is a valve that would be placed on the end of Beckett's tracheostomy tube, allowing air to flow through the vocal cords as well as the nose and mouth. Up until this point, when Beckett took a breath, the air would enter his body at his tracheotomy site in his neck, bypassing his upper airway and nose and mouth altogether. The Passy Muir valve would allow air to flow through the trach, but also into and out of the upper airway through the nose and mouth. The time using the valve would start with maybe thirty minutes, and then eventually work up to all-day use. Once Beckett reached that stage, the team would perform another extensive bronchoscopy and, assuming all looked well, they would then be able to remove his trach. At least, that was the ideal plan.

To say we were anxious for our appointment with the ENT group would be an understatement. We were bursting with anticipation and hope and fear. In late September, we returned to Children's Mercy for our ENT appointment. The ENT specialist—let's call her Dr. W—examined Beckett and then proceeded with the upper airways scope. This was essentially a spaghetti noodle looking device that was fed up through Beckett's nose and down the back of his throat allowing the Doctor to view of the vocal cords and throat/airway above the vocal cords. It was quick, maybe two minutes, but Dr. W did confirm that Beckett's left vocal cord was indeed paralyzed.

Something we had thought was possible but had received contradictory reports on previously. It was likely caused when Beckett had his PDA heart surgery, as it is a common side effect. We were told Beckett would still be able to speak but would likely have a raspy voice.

Next, Dr. W tried the Passy Muir valve on Beckett. This was the big test, the one we needed him to pass so we could start using the valve and move towards decannulation, or trach removal. Dr. W placed the valve on Beckett's trach, and we all watched to see what would happen. Could Beckett breathe using the valve? Would his oxygen saturation rate, which told us how well he was breathing, remain constant? I held my own breath. After less than one minute, it was clear that Beckett was struggling. He squirmed, his face turned red, his oxygen stats fell and so Dr. W removed the valve. My heart sank, and tears filled my eyes, partially because, for the first time ever, I heard Beckett's little voice in the form of a cry as he tried to breathe around the Passy valve, and partially because I knew the easy path, the ideal plan, just went out the window.

Dr. W advised that she wasn't comfortable with Beckett using the valve at home, given his intolerability to it. She explained that she was worried that there was some other obstruction below his vocal cords that she couldn't see with the upper airways scope, which was causing Beckett to not be able to breathe. The obstruction could be scar tissue, a piece of extra skin, a narrowing of his airway or other issues, none of which she could confirm without performing a full bronchoscopy. A bronchoscopy can only be done under anesthesia, meaning they would have to put him under, but would allow for a full scope of the airway, not just the upper airway above the vocal cords. So, a few days after that appointment, we were booked to go off to the operating room once more on October 31st, 2011.

DERAILMENT

At 11:15 a.m. on Tuesday, October 31st, 2011, we arrived at the same-day surgery area at Children's Mercy Hospital for Beckett's 11:30 a.m. appointment. Shortly thereafter, we were moved from the waiting room into a pre-surgery room where we would change Beckett into his surgery gown and be seen by a surgery nurse, anesthesiologist, surgeon, ENT doctor and ENT resident. Again, just as during times before, I would be asked questions about Beckett's medical history. Every time it was a painful reminder of the road we had walked, and yet here we were again. Release forms were signed, and finally around 1:30 p.m., we walked Beckett and the surgery nurse to the entrance of the surgery area. Once there, I handed Beckett to the nurse, kissing him one last time, and he was carried away beyond the doors and into the operating room. It hollowed my heart to watch him be carried away, his big blue eyes peering at me over the nurse's shoulders, clueless to what was waiting for him on the other side of those doors.

We were then sent to the surgery waiting room, the same room we had been in when Beckett was initially transferred to Children's and where we had received the devastating news of him needing a trach just five months earlier. If you've never been in a surgery waiting room, let me describe it for you. Upon arriving, you check in with a receptionist who keeps track of the surgery and contacts you when your child is done with the surgery. At least one parent is usually required to stay in the room at all times, and so the room is equipped with a restroom as well as coffee and snacks. Generally, there are smaller breakout rooms where family members waiting can meet with the doctors and surgeons or receive calls from the operating room nurse with updates on surgery.

About forty-five minutes after Beckett was handed off and sent into the operating room, a surgeon came and met with us in one of the breakout rooms. He was the doctor who had just performed Beckett's circumcision. Yes, you read that correctly. When you're born at twenty-six weeks and survival is all that matters, being circumcised doesn't happen until a later point in life, and for Beckett, this was the day. The doctor advised that everything had gone smoothly with Beckett's circumcision and the ENT doctor was now performing the bronchoscopy. He advised Dr. W (the same ENT we saw at the clinic last month) would come and update us once she was done.

About another forty-five minutes later, Ryan and I were summoned to the small meeting room again. As we waited for Dr. W to arrive, I had a lump in my throat and my heart raced. What she was about to tell us would define Beckett's next steps, his future, our future. It was everything in this moment. She sat down and began to show us pictures taken from the scope of Beckett's airway. There were multiple round pictures on the page, and she explained each one as she spoke about her findings. She was brutally honest with us when she said Beckett's airway was not good. In fact, it was one of the worse ones she had seen. As she pointed to pictures, she explained that Beckett's airway just past his vocal cords and above his trach had so much scar tissue that it was closing off his airway totally, hence why he couldn't tolerate the Passy Muir valve at all. She went on to explain that, in terms of treatment, she would like to wait another six months to see if growth could help open the airway at all and to see how the scar tissue changed, if at all, over that time. The scope that day would give her a baseline for treatment in the future. Regardless, she advised that Beckett would need to have the scar tissue lasered off, likely in multiple treatments and with the use of steroids as well. If that didn't open up his airway to a safe and livable dilatation, then Beckett might need to have a stent building using tissue taken from his ribs and transplanted into his airway to open it up.

Furthermore, Dr. W advised us that, based upon what she saw, she had concerns about if Beckett would have a voice and, if he did, his voice quality. We were aware that he might have a raspy voice, but not that he could sound like he has laryngitis for his entire life. I'm pretty sure Ryan and I stared at her with the same blank look. It felt like deja-vu to when they told us Beckett needed a trach. Dr. W must have realized her brutal honesty and matter-of-fact way of speaking to us left us looking like a deer staring into the headlights of an oncoming car and tried to offer up some compassion, which only caused the tears I had been holding back until that point to rush beyond my eyes and down my face. She reassured Ryan and me that Beckett would not have a trach for the rest of his life. Yes, his airway was in bad shape, but she committed to us that she would help open Beckett's airway. It was just fixing the mechanics of it all.

After pulling myself together, Ryan and I exited the consultation room and found our place back in the main area, waiting for the post-operation nurse to call and let us know when Beckett was done. After about an hour, we asked the receptionist to call the nurse for an update. The nurse advised they were still just working to get Beckett back on "room air," which meant off any supplemental oxygen. Another twenty minutes passed, and we were finally able to head to "Reunion Avenue" and meet Beckett. He was still sedated and sleepy. The nurse showed us his circumcision and how to care for it in the coming days. She removed his IV and explained discharge instructions while I held Beckett. I could tell Beckett was already in pain, and I was, too. When you have children, you will do anything to protect them. Anything. And when you can't, the guilt you feel and the helplessness you carry is torture. Beckett drank some water, which he was able to keep down, a requirement for post-op discharge. And so, we got Beckett dressed and headed home. Him in pain, us in pain and a future path once again unclear.

The week after Beckett's bronchoscopy and circumcision, I allowed myself to sink back into a dark, dark place. It felt like all the progress we had made no longer mattered. I sat at home nursing Beckett back to health and crying about the results of the bronchoscopy. I was mad at life, mad at the world, mad that Beckett had to go through all this. Why us? Why Beckett? Why could nothing seem to go right or easy for us? I saw babies everyday being discharged from the ICN who didn't have to fight through half the hurdles Beckett did. I had friends, co-workers and family members who were announcing their pregnancies and giving birth to healthy babies, none which were delt the cards we were, and I deeply resented them and the universe for that. During this time, I found a piece of literature written in 1987 by Emily Perl Kingsley, called "Welcome to Holland." Emily wrote the essay about her own personal experience in having a child with a disability. Upon reading it, I sat frozen, and I read it again and again. It so perfectly described our plans for Beckett and the reality of Beckett's life since arrival.

Welcome To Holland

by Emily Perl Kingsley

I am often asked to describe the experience of raising a child with a disability - to try to help people who have not shared that unique experience to understand it, to imagine how it would feel. It's like this......

When you're going to have a baby, it's like planning a fabulous vacation trip - to Italy. You buy a bunch of guide books and make your wonderful plans. The Coliseum. The Michelangelo

David. The gondolas in Venice. You may learn some handy phrases in Italian. It's all very exciting.

After months of eager anticipation, the day finally arrives. You pack your bags and off you go. Several hours later, the plane lands. The flight attendant comes in and says, "Welcome to Holland."

"Holland?!?" you say. "What do you mean Holland?? I signed up for Italy! I'm supposed to be in Italy. All my life I've dreamed of going to Italy."

But there's been a change in the flight plan. They've landed in Holland and there you must stay.

The important thing is that they haven't taken you to a horrible, disgusting, filthy place, full of pestilence, famine and disease. It's just a different place.

So you must go out and buy new guide books. And you must learn a whole new language. And you will meet a whole new group of people you would never have met.

It's just a different place. It's slower-paced than Italy, less flashy than Italy. But after you've been there for a while and you catch your breath, you look around.... and you begin to notice that Holland has windmills....and Holland has tulips. Holland even has Rembrandts.

But everyone you know is busy coming and going from Italy... and they're all bragging about what a wonderful time they had there. And for the rest of your life, you will say "Yes, that's where I was supposed to go. That's what I had planned."

And the pain of that will never, ever, ever, ever go away... because the loss of that dream is a very very significant loss.

But... if you spend your life mourning the fact that you didn't get to Italy, you may never be free to enjoy the very special, the very lovely things ... about Holland.

Never in last ten months' time did I find something that I would relate to as much as I could relate to the essay written by Emily. I read and re-read this essay probably 150 times that week after Beckett's surgery. Yes, we had planned Italy, and we thought that our plane had been diverted temporarily, but that we were still on our way to Italy. Now, however, now we were in Holland. And in Holland we would stay for a duration unknown. I hated Holland. And I hated everyone else who was getting to go to Italy. But as I read it again and again, the last lines seemed to resonate louder than the others: "But . . . if you spend your life mourning the fact that you didn't get to Italy, you may never be free to enjoy the very special, the very lovely things . . . about Holland." And so, like before, I forced myself to compartmentalize all those "bad feelings" and focus on the day-to-day positives. Beckett was doing so great in so many other aspects, and so I chose to focus on those and enjoy Beckett where he was, not where I so badly wanted him to be.

As fall turned to winter in Kansas City, Beckett continued to grow and thrive. We took our first road trip with Beckett to Saint Louis to visit my family. I remember being so nervous about it all. I packed about every medical supply we had, including the ventilator and oxygen tanks even though Beckett hadn't needed either in quite some time. Thankfully, we needed none of it, and the trip provided us practice in traveling with Beckett, something which would become much more common soon enough. The holidays came, and despite it being the cold and flu season, and worse for Beckett, the Respiratory Syncytial Virus (RSV) season, we tried to do as much as we could without putting Beckett at risk of catching anything. I was able to secure an early morning private visit to Santa before he was technically open. I remember being so happy to be able to take

Beckett to see Santa. It was something so "normal," and normal was what we wanted more than anything.

We spent Christmas in Iowa with Ryan's family, which almost didn't happen as Beckett came down with a cold about a week before Christmas. It was inevitable that he ended up back on the ventilator due to the increased secretions from an infection in his airway. It was too much for him to handle without some additional breathing support. But after a trip to Children's Mercy where he was treated with an antibiotic, Tussin (cough/mucus depressant), Tylenol and Albuterol, we were back at home to continue to heal. The night of December 22nd, 2011, we all slept on the floor in Beckett's room. On the ventilator, it was easier, with all the cords/tubes, that Beckett sleep in an open area where the tubes could move with him as he rolled in his sleep. In the crib, we had to feed the tubes through the crib slats, and every time Beckett moved or rolled, everything became unhooked or tangled. The next morning, Ryan and I agreed we would head to Iowa. I'm sure people reading this might think we were nuts, traveling five to six hours in the car, in the winter, when our son who was currently on the ventilator was sick, the night after sleeping on the floor with him. Honestly, I think we were a little crazy, too, but at the same time, we agreed when we found out that Beckett would have a trach, that as long as Beckett was safe, we were going to try to live our lives as normal as possible. In essence, we were making a conscious effort to try and enjoy Holland.

Once in Iowa, Beckett's cold continued to improve, and he was off the ventilator by the twenty-fourth. We celebrated Beckett's first Christmas opening gifts, introducing him to more aunts and uncles and cousins and even made another short road trip to Clinton, Iowa, for Beckett to meet more family, but most importantly his great-grandmother. I went alone, just me and Beckett, and despite it only being about a forty-five-minute drive, I had to pull off the highway three times to go to the backseat to suction out Beckett's trach, clearing it of the mucus build up cause from his cold. But the trip was well worth all the effort to get there. As I left Clinton to headed back to Ryan's family's house in Davenport, I was filled with a sense of hope. For once I felt like I was exactly where I was meant to be, with Beckett, surrounded by my family, in my grandparents' home that held so many memories for me and surrounded by so many people who loved me and accepted Beckett as he was. Just being able to travel there was something I had questioned so many times, and yet here we were. We were in Iowa with all our family and Beckett.

The eve of Beckett's first birthday, January 2nd, 2012, I didn't sleep. I remember thinking back to a year ago to that moment . . .

2:21 a.m.: Calling Ryan, being transferred to Saint Luke's on the plaza.

5:15 a.m.: Meeting with NICU nurse and her asking us how much life support we wanted to provide.

6:00 a.m.: Moving to the operating room to deliver.

I was haunted by this day, the day that our lives were forever changed, the day Beckett arrived and, if I am being honest, the nightmare started. Sure, there were moments of happiness and joy, but they were surely overshadowed by all the stress, fear, uncertainty and heartbreak. The past year with Beckett had forced me to master being able to compartmentalize all the bad in order to be able to function or show up as a wife and an employee and a mother and keep going. I hated that. I hated that so much of Beckett's being was associated with "bad feelings" for me. So, on the eve of his first birthday, I unpacked all that shit, every moment and memory etched into my brain, every emotion and feeling, good or bad. I looked back through pictures from our odyssey thus far. I smiled seeing pictures of Ryan's wedding ring, which at the time fit all the way up Beckett's arm, and remembered how Ryan lost his wedding ring in the hospital parking garage for a day before we amazingly found it. I cried when I remembered Beckett's multiple failures at being extubated and him coding. I felt hope when I remembered all the family, friends, coworkers and complete strangers who made us meals, sent us cards, gave us money and carried us through the last twelve months. I laughed remembering joyful moments with some of our favorite nurses and doctors along the way. And then, once I had sorted through all the contents of all those boxes, I repacked all of it and closed the door on it for good. No more dwelling, no more pity parties about the past and how we got here. We were in Holland, and we were going to enjoy it there for as long as we needed to, even if that meant forever.

STARTING AGAIN

The year 2012 hit us like a bullet train, and each day we traveled at warp speed. When nightfall came and we caught our breaths, we would look around to see what was left of ourselves. My career seemed relentless at the time, with increased workload, travel agendas and work drama. Ryan was gone more than he was home with his job, which left me relying heavily on an unreliable nanny for Beckett. She would call in and say she couldn't make it for the day fifteen minutes after she was supposed to be there or show up thirty to forty-five minutes late with no call to let me know she was on her way. It was so stressful. And unfortunately, that stress manifested itself into blame against Ryan for being gone the majority of the time. We fought often, and when I got tired of the same argument, I resorted to silence. So many nights Ryan would call me from Dallas, where he was usually entertaining clients or out with coworkers, and while his intentions were good, I hated him. I would barely say five words as I resented him for being in Dallas and out for dinners or drinks (all necessities of his work) while I was barely able to keep afloat with my days. Our relationship was crumbling apart, and truly it was the last thing I had any effort to save.

To add more shit to-do, on top of the existing pile of shit to-do, I had also started to research what the findings from Beckett's bronchoscopy in October might mean. At that time, Dr. W, the ENT from Children's Mercy, advised that Beckett had stage III subglottic stenosis. Subglottic stenosis is a narrowing of the airway in part of the voice box below the vocal cords.

Stage IV is the worse, so I knew that treatment wasn't likely to be an easy fix, but more likely a major surgery. Dr. W's plan was to do a bronchoscopy for Beckett again in April and see if his growth had changed his airway at all. April seemed like a long time to wait just to see what's next. Thus, off to the innerwebs I went to see what I could find. And, if you've ever asked Dr. Google for medical advice, you know you will find about every possible solution for your issue. I found all sorts of articles and publications on the topic, but it wasn't until I found a YouTube video produced by The Children's Hospital of Philadelphia (CHOP) titled "Introduction to Airway Disorders and Our Pediatric Airway Center" that I felt like I had found something viable. The video highlighted a baby similar to Beckett, born early and unable to be extubated, thus receiving a tracheotomy. It walked through her treatment at CHOP with the airway team.

I'm not sure if I shared this video with my parents or if it was their medical backgrounds that encouraged me to seek a second opinion on Beckett's diagnosis and treatments plan. At the time, we had all faith in Children's Mercy, but given that Beckett's diagnosis was more severe than we original thought and that it would likely require a complex surgery, we wanted to validate that they were on track with one of the nationally renowned airway programs like those at CHOP or Cincinnati Children's. So, with my mom's help, I collected all the documents needed and sent a packet off to CHOP for them to review. In early February of 2012, I received a call from Rosemary Patel, a Nurse Practitioner from the ENT airway team at CHOP. They had received Beckett's medical records, and she needed to review some items with me. I spent about an hour going through Beckett's medical history with her and answering questions she had. She advised that the information would be passed along to Dr. Ian Jacobs, director and ENT airway surgeon, for his review.

About a week later, Ryan and I participated in a conference call with Dr. Jacobs to talk about the airway program at CHOP and his review of Beckett's records. From the start, Ryan and I were impressed by Dr. Jacobs' dedication to his patients. After all, he had agreed to start the call at 9:00

p.m. his time in order to meet both Ryan and my other commitments (i.e., client dinners and me getting Beckett down for bed) and to dial into a conference call number since Ryan was in Dallas and I was in Kansas City. Dr. Jacobs started by describing how treatment works at CHOP, with it being interdisciplinary and involving other specialties such as pulmonology and GI, to name a few. He advised the number of cases, similar to Beckett's, that he had operated on, the decannulation success rates and what the process of airway reconstruction would look like. Furthermore, Ryan and I were put at ease by his willingness to answer any questions we had, and we never felt rushed by him, even though it was pushing 10:00 p.m. his time towards the end of the call. I remember just feeling so reassured speaking to someone who was clearly such an expert in this field.

In order for CHOP to really give us a fully evaluation and treatment plan, they of course wanted to see Beckett in person. After the call with Dr. Jacobs, we tentatively scheduled appointments at CHOP for April 26th and 27th, 2012. However, we knew that travel to and from CHOP would not only be difficult, but also expensive so we wanted to meet with the ENT group at Children's Mercy in Kansas City once again to validate if we felt they were on the same level with CHOP now that we had a better understanding of Beckett's diagnosis and potential surgery needs and make our decision after that.

On February 21st, 2012, I took Beckett to Children's Mercy for an appointment with the ENT group there. We once again saw Dr. W who has been the same physician from the ENT group, we saw both in the Home Ventilator Clinic where she performed an upper airway scope, and we tried the Passy Muir valve in late September 2011 and who performed a full bronchoscopy on Beckett on October 31st, 2011 – in short this wasn't Beckett's first time with Dr. W. Upon arrival, we waited patiently in the waiting room before being placed into an exam room. Dr. W seemed very flustered and rushed when she came into the room to meet Beckett and me. We started talking, and I told her I had some questions regarding the last bronchoscopy she did in October. I wanted to know what Beckett's range was, in terms of a percentage, of stenosis in his airway. Annoyed with the question, Dr. W advised that she didn't know the percentage because they didn't pull all the records for her appointments and then frustratingly logged into the computer in the room to try and confirm. I was annoyed. Shouldn't she be prepared for my questions or at least welcoming of them and willing to find the answer? Isn't that the entire reason for the appointment? I further elaborated that we were interested to know if Beckett was at the lower end grade (71 percent) of stage III subglottic stenosis or the upper end grade (90 percent), as we had heard it makes a difference in required surgery and decannulation success rates.

Dr. W explained as she looked at the computer that she could not advise an exact percentage like 23 percent versus 25 percent. I could understand that, but still saw it as a red flag that she wasn't giving me a percentage range. Upon reviewing the computer records, she advised that Beckett was actually 57 to 60 percent, which wasn't even stage III at all. It was stage II (51 to 71 percent). She said her colleague must have mistyped it at the time and she was making a note to have it corrected in the system. *Awesome*, I thought to myself, *there goes my confidence in her and this ENT team.*

We continued to talk regarding what her plan would be for Beckett. She advised that she would like to do a bronchoscopy again in late March or early April. She said she didn't have a crystal ball to be able to tell her findings at the time, but advised that, if he did need a major reconstruction surgery, she would not consider it now as he was too young for it. Another red flag for me—CHOP had advised that age does not play a role if surgery is possible; size, yes, not age. Dr. W further advised that she would like more time to allow Beckett to grow. Generally, she said she doesn't not perform such large operations until three to four years of age. Therefore, in the meantime, her plan would be to perform a bronchoscopy every six months on Beckett until he was ready for surgery. She made some reference to ensuring that he was not refluxing, but made no mention of bringing in additional specialties such as Gastrointestinal (GI), pulmonology, anesthesia or Speech Therapy (ST) or Occupational Therapy (OT) into the care plan. Another red flag for me based on what Dr. Jacobs had described as CHOP's care plan for airway surgery.

At this point, she seemed to be annoyed that we were even talking about surgery and said something to the effect of we really shouldn't even have this conversation until a year or so from now. I explained that I understood that; however, Ryan and I felt blindsided to learn of the stage III subglottic stenosis diagnosis last October, and we wanted to ensure that we understood all potential surgeries/outcomes and we also wanted to ensure we were making the best decisions for him regarding care. And now, given that the stage III diagnosis wasn't even correct, and she was treating me with zero professionalism, I was getting angry. Wasn't she supposed to be a consultant to me and help me by answering these questions? Why was she annoyed that I was trying to understand the medical diagnosis and treatment options in an effort to be the best advocate for Beckett's care? I wasn't questioning her credentials, just looking for answers.

I also asked how many cases like Beckett she had seen. She advised that she personally only performed major reconstructive surgeries on four to six patients a year. She had been in practice for eight years. She also advised that as an ENT practice they did many more since there were eight to nine pediatric ENT physicians at Children's Mercy. She advised that she had only had one major reconstructive failure where the tissues from the ribs used to build the airway stent died and the trach had to be put back in. Further frustrating in our conversation, she went back and reviewed the results from Beckett's original bronchoscopy in March 2011 when he received his trach shortly after our transfer to Children's Mercy. In that report, the ENT doctor (unknown) had advised that Beckett had severe swelling near his vocal cords, but that his subglottic was clear, so there was no evidence of stenosis at that time. Dr. W said she doubted these findings as he clearly had subglottic stenosis now and putting a trach in should not cause subglottic stenosis, especially not to the degree that Beckett had it. I sat in shock, like what the actual fuck was happening? My mind was blown on so many levels. Had Beckett been misdiagnosed before he even received his trach? What are we doing here? And what have we been doing all this time?

I was frustrated and angry and honestly didn't know what to think or believe in that moment. I said we can schedule time for a bronchoscopy in late March or early April as she wanted, but that we did need to have a bigger trach put in that day. Dr. W hollered into the hallway about needing a scope and assistance in the room. We moved into the next exam room that had a table to lay Beckett on for the trach change/new trach. At this point, Dr. W apologized to me if she seemed flustered that day. She explained that she was not feeling well, her child was sick and they had a new puppy at home. I said it was no problem, but in reality, what I wanted to ask her was if in the last thirteen months she had delivered a baby at twenty-six weeks, who spent five months in the hospital and had to deal with physicians like herself to try to get the best care for her child? *Your life with a cold, minorly ill child and puppy is not that rough, lady.*

I assisted her with the trach change along with two other nurses. She advised that Beckett's stoma site (place on the neck where the trach enters the airway) looked great. No granulation tissue was present. Once the new trach was secured, she scoped his trach and said the fit looked good. She also stuck the scope down Beckett's nose and advised that she believed his vocal cords looked better than in October when she had performed the last scope. Potentially good news, but by this point her words held no weight with me. When Dr. W was done, she wrote down the name of a colleague at Cincinnati Children's along with her email and said to email her any additional questions Ryan or I might have. Beckett and I packed up and left the exam room to sit in the scheduler's waiting room to make an appointment for the bronchoscopy. But after waiting for ten minutes, we just left without making an appointment. I was done. And needless to say, that was our last appointment with the ENT group at Children's Mercy. We would be pursuing CHOP for our airway care from that point onward.

March 2012 broke me, like really broke me. My relationship with Ryan was hanging on by strings. I felt that he was prioritizing work over me, and Beckett and I resented him for that. I was dying a slow death trying to keep up with all things, and he was fine flying in a silver bullet each week away from us with no hesitation. There was no relationship between us. Yes, we still lived together and co-parented on the weekends. We were still trying to march Beckett's medical care forward together, but we were both miserable. By mid-March, it all came to a head, and all the weight and hate and anger and frustrations and pain crashed along with it. I lay in bed for a week, Ryan was back on the road in Dallas and my mom was in town to help care for Beckett since our first nanny was let go as she never showed up or was constantly late anyway. I wanted to do nothing, see no one. I wanted to cry and cave into my misery. I felt numb, like what do you do when literally every aspect of your life is going bad or wrong or is so dang hard? Which piece do you pick up first to try to start again? How do you find the strength to keep going? I don't remember magically finding the answers to all or any of those questions, nor do I recall what ultimately got me out of bed and motivated to try to move life forward again. But maybe that's just it: Sometimes you just have to get up and show up. Even if you don't know how or what you are doing, or why you are doing it, you just show up. And that's all the start you need.

THE ROAD MAP

By April, we had secured a new nanny for Beckett, and so I was back on the usual rigmarole: keeping up with my career, staying on top of Beckett's care and therapies, working on Ryan and I's relationship, the house, the dog and so on. In addition, I was also finalizing our plans for Beckett's trip to CHOP to be evaluated by the airway team. Living in Kansas City and traveling to Philadelphia wasn't exactly a cake walk. It involved airplane tickets, rental car reservations, booking hotels in a foreign city and then there was the coordination of appointments at CHOP. We were to be seen by four specialties in clinical appointments and then would go to the OR for a bronchoscopy the next day. That was just the logistics of it all. Then you have to remember the packing and actual travel. While I was very excited to meet with the team at CHOP, the idea of flying with Beckett was terrifying: One because of just the amount of crap we would be bringing— clothing and usual stuff, but also medical equipment and supplies and food for Beckett—and two, not knowing how Beckett would respond to flying with the changes in the cabin pressure, potential exposure to germs during travel and so on. To add to the stress, a day or so before we were scheduled to leave, Ryan and I came down with cold. So, we masked up with surgical masks when at home and around Beckett and made sure to disinfect everything in an effort to keep the germs away from Beckett.

On Wednesday, April 25th, 2012, we boarded a big metal bird at Kansas City International Airport. With Beckett having a medical condition, we were able to obtain a pre-board authorization, but even with that, Ryan and I were in a full sweat with racing hearts by the time we sat down on the plane. We brought Lysol spray and wipes and literally bombed the row we decided to sit in. We carried Beckett's car seat and placed him in the window seat. Buckling the seat into the airplane and Beckett into the seat, we situated all the emergency medical equipment within arm's reach should we need to suction Beckett, change a trach or God forbid hook him back up to the ventilator while in flight. Thankfully, we touched down in Philadelphia without any issues. I'll never forget the lady sitting in front of Beckett during the flight turning back and saying, "Wow, he did *so* great on the flight. I never even heard him make a peep!" I just smiled and said thank you. Little did she know he couldn't make a peep if he wanted to.

We made our way from the plane to the baggage area to claim our overweight bag we had to pay an additional $50 for because of all the extra medical crap we had to bring. From there, we boarded the rental car bus, got our rental car, and finally made it to our hotel. Our appointments with CHOP didn't start until the next day, and so we had the afternoon and evening to rest and recover from the stress of traveling.

The next day, we arrived at CHOP for our first appointment with Dr. Jacobs. It was so great to meet with him and Rosemary, our nurse practitioner from the airway team at CHOP, in person. We reviewed some medical history, and then he performed an upper airway scope (aka slipping a spaghetti noodle sized camera up Beckett's nose and down the back of his throat to view his upper airway). Beckett had this type of scope done many times in Kansas City, but it was always just the doctor looking into the scope; here it was projected onto a large computer screen, which was awesome because, for the first time, I could see and understand what was going on, as well.

From the scope, Dr. Jacobs confirmed that both Beckett's vocal cords were in fact moving and not paralyzed, which was fantastic news. However, he also advised that Beckett's adenoids were very large and would likely have to be removed prior to any airway reconstructive surgery being performed. During the scope, there was also a speech therapist in the room, and while the scope was down, we were able to coax Beckett into drinking a little green-dyed milk. She was able to confirm that she saw no issues with his ability to swallow, also good news. We measured Beckett's expiratory pressure while using the speaking valve and, from that, were advised to discontinue the use of the valve for now. Finally, we learned that Beckett would stay inpatient one night after his bronchoscopy, which was scheduled for the next day (Friday morning), as the Gastroenterology (GI) team would be placing an impedance probe to measure acid and non-acid reflux into the esophagus for about twenty-four hours. This is a critical thing to be aware of as you don't want to have any reflex coming up after a reconstructive surgery damaging any already fragile transplanted tissues.

From there, we met with Dr. Maqbool, the GI doctor, and spoke through the procedure for the next day, which would be an upper endoscopy with biopsies and the placement of the impedance probe. Dr. Jacobs would first complete the bronchoscopy of Beckett's airway, and then Dr. Maqbool would perform his scope, biopsy and placement of the probe. After concluding with our GI appointment and signing more release papers for the procedure, we had about an hour to kill before our next appointments.

We headed to an Au Bon Pain restaurant near the Wood Center Building, which was where all of our appointments were. The weather was cool and rainy. By this time, Beckett was exhausted from getting up early and being probed and poked and prodded and had fallen asleep in the stroller. Ryan and I ate an early lunch and tried to relax a bit. The entire trip thus far had been exhausting on all levels. Traveling with Beckett, navigating a foreign city, lack of sleep, fighting a cold and then add on the stress of going from appointment to appointment, it was physically and mentally draining. Not only that, but the emotional toll was tremendous, as well. Holding Beckett down for exams, trying to take in and understand what Beckett's prognosis was for each doctor/specialty and then seeing some of the sickest kids we'd ever seen in each hallway and waiting room, it was heart wrenching and quite honestly depressing. By the time we headed to our next appointment, I could tell Ryan was struggling, and I was, too. I found myself in disbelief that we were at CHOP and that this was "our" lives. I started going down the "why me?" road in my head and immediately made a U-turn. Nothing good was going to come from that road that day, and besides, I had two more appointments to focus on and get through.

Next was anesthesia, which was nothing different than the million other times we had gone to surgery with Beckett: review of medical history and signing of release forms. Our final appointment was with pulmonology and Dr. Piccione. Once again, we reviewed medical history, reviewed the procedures for the next day, bronchoscopy and bronchoalveolar. Dr. Piccione was very kind, and I was excited to hear that he had recently come to CHOP from Cincinnati Children's. Cincinnati Children's was the other facility we were going to pursue a second opinion from as they are another center of excellence for pediatric airway reconstruction. So, I was happy to know Dr. Piccione would be bringing his experience from that facility to Beckett's case as well.

Around 2:00 p.m., we returned to the hotel for the day, once again exhausted but ready for the next day to come. I called the surgery line to obtain our arrival time for the next morning, a practice which would become so familiar that I still have the number saved in my cell phone contacts today. We were to arrive at the pre-surgery area at 6:15 a.m. So early, but I was thankful for that as Beckett wouldn't be able to eat or drink anything before the procedure and that's not an easy thing to explain to a fifteen-month-old, who is used to eating at set times. Morning came quickly, and by 7:00 a.m., we were placed into a pre-surgery waiting room where we put Beckett in his surgery gown and waited for Dr. Jacobs and the anesthesiologist to come speak with us. After giving Beckett a bit of "giggle juice" to help him relax, I once again placed him in the arms of one of the surgery nurses and watched as he was carried through the secure double doors into the surgery corridor. From there, Ryan and I were moved into the surgery waiting room. We settled in, and about thirty minutes later, a nurse came and advised the pulmonology procedure was complete and Dr. Jacobs was starting his procedures. We then received a call from Dr. Jacobs from surgery that he had found a rather large polyp in Beckett's airway and requested consent to remove it. Ryan and I agreed, and then we waited some more. Finally, at about 10:00 a.m., Ryan and I were moved from the surgery waiting room and placed into a conference room. There we were met with all three of the doctors and specialties who performed procedures on Beckett. They informed us of the following:

- Ears, Nose and Throat - ENT (Dr. Jacobs): Beckett possessed a stage II stenosis of the airway, which will require an anterior and posterior graph through reconstructive surgery of his airway which will be completed in two phases or separate surgeries. Overall, Dr. Jacobs felt like Beckett was a great candidate for surgery and that the first surgery could take place as early as September 2012, with decannulation (or trach removal) taking place three to nine months after that.

- Pulmonology (Dr. Piccione): Beckett possessed tracheomalacia, which basically meant, in addition to the stenosis of the airway, he had a "floppy" airway. There was no treatment for the condition, but with growth it would become less of an inhabitant for Beckett. We would have to wait for lab results on the biopsies and cultures that they obtained during surgery.

- Gastroenterology - GI (Dr. Maqbool): Everything looked normal for Beckett and the PH probe was placed and would remain in until 9:30 a.m. the next day, at which point once removed, we would have a better idea if Beckett had any reflux. We needed to be aware of and treat it as a part of his reconstructive surgery care plan.

When the doctors left, Ryan and I were moved back to the surgery waiting room, and we waited for the recovery nurse to call us and let us know that we could come back and see Beckett. As we waited, Ryan and I discussed the findings the doctors shared with us. While it was along the lines of what we thought might be needed, it was the first time *ever* we finally felt like we could see the road on the map leading us to where we needed to go. Sure, there were still so many unknowns, but we were finally confident in the care team and diagnosis and felt like we were exactly where we needed to be with being at CHOP. Soon we were called back to the post-op area, and while my heart leaped to see my boy, it was soon breaking as I watched Beckett struggle to come out of the anesthesia. Previously he had recovered pretty well when coming out of surgeries, but this time he was vomiting, had a high heart rate, respiratory rate and unstable oxygen saturation rates. Finally, around 2:00 p.m., we were able to give him some milk that he kept down, but when we tried to give him some Tylenol a few hours later, that came right back up. We decided to administer him some Zofran and, in the process of waiting for that to come from the pharmacy, took Beckett's temperature and realized that he had spiked a temperature of 103°. A spike in temperature is not uncommon after an operation, but still not fun.

By afternoon, Beckett was placed in his overnight room within the hospital, and Ryan and I were at the ends of our ropes trying to console an inconsolable Beckett. We tried everything—rocking, holding, reading, singing, toys, videos—anything to help him find comfort, but nothing was working. I'm sure he felt like shit, had a sore throat from the polyp removal, a pounding headache from the fever and was annoyed by the probe running to his stomach, which I can't say that I blame him for, but as a parent you feel so much guilt, guilt for agreeing to do all this and putting him under anesthesia and through another procedure, and now helplessness as there was absolutely nothing we could do to help him feel better except to be there and keep trying all things. Finally, we asked the nurse to administer something stronger for pain and to help him become more comfortable. A dose of morphine took the edge off a little, but not much.

By 7:15 p.m., he was starting to work himself into another frenzy. Ryan and I had planned to run down to the hospital cafeteria to get some dinner before they closed at 8:00 p.m., but before we knew it, the time had almost passed. We decided that I would run down and grab something for both of us. Mind you, CHOP is a very large hospital and one in which I had to obtain directions from the nurse, which involved riding down two different sets of elevators and making a number of different lefts and rights to actually arrive at the right place. I made it all the way to the cafeteria entrance only to find it was already closed. I lost it. Big tears streamed down my face, and while I turned and tried to hold it together, I was a mess. So much so I could barely read the signs through my tears and find my way back to Beckett's room. When I arrived, Ryan and I held each other, both needing a hug more than I think we knew. After a good cry, I felt like I had removed the huge elephant of stress from the past couple of days that had been riding on my shoulders. We were able to find a nearby pizza joint that would deliver to the hospital, and we finally ate some dinner around 10:00 p.m. We decided that Ryan would head back to the hotel and I would stay with Beckett at the hospital that night. While I really needed sleep, I also knew that I could never leave Beckett alone at the hospital, and if I did, I would not sleep anyway because I would worry about him all night, so I was better off staying at his bedside.

The night was uneventful except for Beckett waking every two hours. I think he was freaked out from being somewhere he didn't know and likely still uncomfortable from the procedures too. That and, let's be honest, no one sleeps in the hospital. I did feed him at 12:00 a.m. and 5:00 a.m. without issue, and by sunrise his temperature had finally broken. The oncoming day, the nurse was able to remove Beckett's IV, which also meant we could remove his "no-nos" that were essentially braces they put on his arms to keep him from being able to bend his arms so he couldn't pull out his IVs or probes. By midmorning, he was off the remaining half liter of oxygen support he was receiving, and by 12:00 p.m., the GI doctor arrived to remove his probe, at which point we were discharged. We were scheduled to fly home Saturday, the day we were discharged. However, when Dr. Jacobs removed the polyp from Beckett's airway, he advised it would be best if we could wait an additional day to travel home. Thus, we altered our flights to fly home on Sunday and due to flight times made the decision to drive from Philadelphia to Baltimore and fly from Baltimore back to Kansas City. The bad news was we would now have a two-hour drive from Philadelphia to Baltimore, and the good news was that our flight home would now be direct.

You would have thought the flight home to Kansas City would have been much less stressful than the flight out, but that was not the case. I was so worried about Beckett knowing that Dr. Jacobs removed a polyp from his airway. While we were cleared to fly home, I was still anxious about it causing issues and, seeing how much he struggled to recover from the procedure and knowing he was still not 100 percent back to himself also had me on edge.

We made it to Baltimore without issue, returned the rental car, navigated our way through the new airport and eventually onto the plane. I had a bottle ready for Beckett that I fed him once we were all settled in our seats and ready for take-off. He took the bottle well, but then moments later the entire thing came back up. I panicked. He was strapped into his five-point car seat, and mind you, his airway was under his chin. I went into survival mode, pushing Beckett's head as far forward as possible while being strapped in and using burp rags and blankets to attempt to catch all the vomit. By the time it was over, we were wheels up, and I had successfully kept him from aspirating and had caught the majority of the mess. I gave him a suction to clear his airway of congestion, and before I could finish, he was asleep. He was exhausted. I was exhausted. We all were exhausted. I melted into Ryan in the seat next to me and tried to finally relax the rest of the flight home.

About a week later, the results from all the biopsies and tests that were run at CHOP started to roll in. All in all, everything was checking out as normal. Dr. Piccione, the pulmonologist, did report that Beckett had three different bacteria present in his lungs, which would be treated with antibiotics. But that was about it. The next step would be to wait for the care teams we met with at CHOP to have a case review regarding Beckett's case. From there, a care plan would be developed. It was the beginning of June when we finally received a concrete plan of care for Beckett. We learned that Beckett would in fact need his airway rebuilt, and that would happen over a series of surgeries. The tentative plan was as follows:

August 3rd, 2012 - Adenoidectomy and Tonsillectomy Surgery: We would return to CHOP for Beckett to have his adenoids and tonsils removed. They were both large and removing them would help open up his already small airway. In addition, Dr. Jacobs would perform another bronchoscopy, and Dr. Piccione would do some additional pre-reconstructive pulmonology testing while there. We could have elected to have this surgery completed in Kansas City; however we felt most comfortable in keeping everything with one surgeon and one care team even though it was immensely inconvenient and expensive to travel to CHOP for care.

September 6th, 2012 - Double Stage Laryngotracheal Reconstructive (LTR) Surgery: Assuming all would go well with the adenoid and tonsil removal in August, Beckett would be scheduled for a double stage LTR surgery in September. The simple version of what this surgery entails would be this. They would harvest rib graph tissue from Beckett's rib cage. They would use that tissue and place it in his airway in the area where his airway was compromised to help open it up more, making it both wider and also stronger. A horizontal incision would be made in his neck to access his airway and then would be closed back up. His trach would still remain intact even after the surgery. That's why it is called a double stage LTR, because even after the graph placement, he would still have and need his trach to breathe.

Unknown Date - Single Stage Laryngotracheal Reconstructive (LTR) Surgery: The timing of this surgery was unknown, but would be needed once Beckett was completely healed from the double stage LTR and once Dr. Jacobs felt like Beckett was ready for decannulation, which meant trach removal. With the single stage LTR, it was essentially the same surgery as the double stage, rib graph harvest and placement within the airway. However, with the single stage LTR, the trach would be removed as part of the surgery.

Finally having a plan for surgery and eventual decannulation felt amazing. We now had a map, knew where our destination was and where the necessary stops along the way would be. And so, the planning began, and there was so much to figure out.

Like all time since Beckett was born, time seemed to crawl past. The days were filled with the balance of work and Beckett's care, and we tried to have a little bit of summer fun too. The funny thing about having a medically compromised child is you try to give them as normal of a life as possible, but in your mind, some worst-case scenario is always playing out. We played cautiously in a kiddie pool in the backyard, went to places like the park and aquarium, armed with Lysol spray, Lysol wipes and hand sanitizer long before the pandemic days where it became normal to look like a hypochondriac. We got tons of looks as we sprayed down the park swings and slides and feverishly sanitized Beckett's hands as he touched everything as most toddlers do.

The other hard thing, especially as a mother, was to watch how other kids and even parents engaged with Beckett. From afar, he looked like a typical toddler, but up close, they would notice the trach. And when other kids would try to talk to Beckett, he of course could say nothing in return. Some kids and parents would disengage immediately; others had a million questions about what was "wrong" with him and so on. Either way, as a parent, it was heartbreaking.

Along those same lines, I'll never forget the time I met up with two friends, both of whom were pregnant and expecting babies of their own, to go garage sale shopping. I'll never forget how much of an outsider I felt like, as they discussed what they should bring to the hospital and which bedding would be best, and so on and so forth. Meanwhile, I pushed Beckett along in a stroller with all his medical equipment thinking to myself none of what they were discussing really mattered. What mattered was delivering a healthy baby, nothing more and nothing less. It didn't matter what you packed in your hospital bag or what baby items were the best. All you *really* need is a healthy baby. That was everything. Even now that we somewhat knew our destination with Beckett, this interaction was a reminder of that broken dream of having a healthy baby, and it stung bad.

FINDING OUR PACE

Finally, the calendar turned to August 1st, 2012, and we boarded another airplane east bound. We arrived in Baltimore without issue and drove to Philadelphia. On this trip, we opted for the drive from Baltimore to Philadelphia versus a connecting flight directly into Philadelphia. That evening, we checked into our hotel and got settled. After I got Beckett to sleep in the hotel room, I went to the small kitchenette area to talk to Ryan who was trying to prepare for a client interview at a new client site. As I sat down, he handed me a card and box of chocolates. It was my 30th birthday. I remember feeling so sad in that moment. There we sat in a hotel room hundreds of miles away from home and all our friends and family and preparing for yet another surgical procedure for our baby boy. No special birthday dinner, no gifts and no time with family and friends to celebrate. Needless to say, my 30th birthday was one of my least favorite one's ever. The next morning, a Thursday, Beckett would be seen by Dr. Jacobs in the clinic to ensure everything still looked good, and assuming it did, Friday morning he would head to the operating room.

Our Thursday morning appointments went without any reason to delay surgery, and we were set for Friday. We spent the remainder of the afternoon walking around the University of Pennsylvania campus, which our hotel was located close to. I watched as Beckett walked and ran through the manicured walkways along the historic large stone and brick buildings. He would stop and squat to look at a fallen leaf or rock, and then he was off again. He loved pushing along the umbrella stroller although he was a terrible driver. I remember my heart aching as I watched him wander about without a care in the world. He had absolutely no idea what was coming the next day, and that broke my heart. I wish there was some way I could tell him, and he would understand, tell him that the next day and the coming months were going to be painful and quite honestly miserable, but in the long run that everything would be okay, tell him so he could understand and could prepare himself, tell him so he knew there was a reason for the pain and suffering, but I knew that there was no way to do that. And then again as I watched him, I thought maybe it was his innocence and unknowing of what was to come that would make all this easier on him. As his mother, I just prayed this was the case and he would have no memory of all the pain that he had experienced and would experience in the future.

On Friday, we arrived at the pre-surgery area at CHOP at 10:15 a.m. As I learned from many surgical procedures with Beckett, usually a combination of the youngest patients and most urgent or critical surgeries get the earlier arrival times, and while 10:15 a.m. was better for sleeping in, it was terrible for not being able to eat and experiencing operating room delays. And that proved to be the case for surgery that day. About an hour after arriving, we were placed in a pre-surgery room. These rooms are similar to what you would find if you went to an emergency room, just a small room where they prep you and hold you until the operating room is ready for your case. Thankfully, Beckett was a pretty chill toddler and remained entertained by the TV and toys brought in by the child life specialist and eventually fell asleep in my arms. When the operating room nurse came to take Beckett, I gently placed him in her arms, both Ryan and I kissing his head, and we watched as he was carried through the double doors, we had watched him go through before. It was 1:30 p.m. by that point.

Ryan and I checked into the surgery waiting area and waited for an update from Dr. Jacobs. I can't remember how long the surgery took, but they always seemed longer than they actually were. We were eventually told by the waiting room receptionist to go to one of the private rooms, and we waited for Dr. Jacobs to come speak with us. He arrived and advised that he was able to successfully remove both Beckett's tonsils and adenoids without any issues. That was the update we expected to hear, but what we didn't expect was the following news. Dr. Jacobs advised that the tissue in Beckett's airway looked inflamed and "active." He advised that he wasn't sure if it was from a recent ear infection Beckett had, but said that because of the inflamed tissue, he wasn't sure that the Double Stage LTR surgery planned for September would still be possible.

Like all unfavorable news regarding Beckett, my mind started running a million miles an hour, and suddenly I couldn't remember what I was going to just ask the doctor or what the last thing he just said was. Thankfully, Ryan's brain operates in a very calm and logical manner, and he was able to ask the right questions while I sat there feeling like I was chasing a butterfly with my thoughts. Dr. Jacobs further advised that they ran a gram stain as well as a viral panel, and if one of those came back showing the cause of the inflammation and we could treat it right away, then the Double Stage LTR surgery in September could still be possible. Once we were finished speaking with Dr. Jacobs, we were led up to the pediatric intensive care unit (PICU) where Beckett was already moved to from surgery and to the room he would remain until discharged. Ryan and I expected the worse with post-op and recovery given how Beckett came out of anesthesia in April, but much to our surprise, this recovery didn't seem to be going any worse, and we welcomed that.

Recovery from any surgery has this natural progression that occurs, and over time, it became a song and dance that I knew well. First the focus was on watching for any red flags or major issues that could be life threatening or compromise the surgery. Comfort is key immediately post-surgery as the anesthesia is wearing off and pain management is needed. This is a highly stressful part of recovery and one where I feel like as a mom you are constantly on edge and holding your breath for. Once you are past this critical stage, then you want to start focusing on slowly removing the support put into place because of the surgery, for example, moving from being fully ventilator dependent to just an oxygen supplement to breathing independently, or to go from being fed via a feeding tube or receiving TPN (nutrients given via an IV) to partially eating orally to eating all food by mouth and receiving no nutrients by IV or feeding device. And these were exactly the stages we followed for Beckett.

By Friday evening, Beckett was still on the ventilator, being sustained by IV nutrients and receiving morphine via IV and Tylenol suppositories for pain. We also found out later on Friday that one of the gram stains came back positive, and Beckett was started on a medication called Bactrim to help fight the infection. By Saturday morning, Beckett was removed from the ventilator and was breathing on his own. This was a huge relief as getting stuck on the ventilator again was always a near thought in my mind. They also turned off his IV nutrients in an effort to make him feel thirstier and hungrier and want to try to eat something orally. Also, on Saturday, we found out that the culture taken during surgery tested positive for rhinovirus, which is just the common cold. While we were thankful it wasn't anything more serious, it was also frustrating as there is really nothing to help "cure" a cold. Like all viruses, it just has to run its course.

Sunday morning found me with bloodshot eyes after being with Beckett at the hospital since Friday morning when we arrived for surgery. Again, there was no point in both Ryan and I staying, and since I would just worry all night should I return to the hotel, I opted to stay with Beckett the entire time, a necessity for my worrying mind to know what was always going on and to see him 24/7 to validate that, but 100 percent physically and emotionally draining. Thankfully, by Sunday afternoon, we were approved for discharge. Pain prescriptions in hand, which we filled at the outpatient pharmacy located inside of CHOP, we made our way back to our hotel.

On Monday, we were able to fly back home, but once again, I had never been so nervous and had so much anxiety to fly with Beckett. If you have ever known anyone who's had their tonsils removed, then you know one of the biggest risk factors is post-surgical bleeding, and it's terrifying.

Add onto that being in a foreign city, traveling and having a child with an already compromised airway, who is nonverbal, and it's nearly beyond what you can handle. All I could envision was being thirty thousand feet in the air and realizing Beckett was bleeding and trying to get help fast enough. Awful, it was awful.

Thankfully, we did make it home without incident, but recovery for Beckett was far from over. We had been dosing him every four hours with his prescription pain medication to keep him comfortable and try to keep him eating and drinking, but it was a slow process and I feared he would start dropping weight since he was only taking in about 50 percent of what he was eating before surgery. He was also constipated, a side effect from the pain meds, drooled a ton because who wants to swallow when your throat is raw and wasn't sleeping well, which meant I wasn't sleeping either. Both my parents ended up coming to Kansas City in rotating shifts to help me continue to nurse Beckett back to health. And slowly, and painfully, we did. It was near the end of August, but Beckett was finally over his cold and had recovered from his surgery.

About that time, we also learned that Beckett's first major airway reconstructive surgery would be pushed from September 4th to October 4th, just to give Beckett a little more time to heal and ensure the tissues in his airway weren't inflamed or had any residual swelling from having his tonsils and adenoids removed or from the cold. While this was another setback, knowing the complexity of the reconstructive surgery and how important it was to ensure everything was as perfect as possible before-hand, I welcomed the delay.

As August turned to September, we were able to accomplish a few things with Beckett I had been wanting to do. One was we had Beckett bap-tized, something I had wanted to do when he was younger, but never felt he was stable enough or that the time was right to risk his exposure to germs by taking him into the church setting. Not that churches are dirty, but we really didn't take Beckett out many places in public and, if we did, were *very* cautious. We also had some family pictures taken, another thing which most people do frequently with babies or toddlers, but something we had never done. Beckett was at the perfect age and had a smile that would melt anyone's heart, and with it still being summertime, we could take pictures outdoors, which was even better to limit germ exposure.

By the time September rolled around, we had imposed a self-quarantine to reduce the risk of Beckett being exposed to any germs that could cause him to get sick and ultimately result in another delay in his scheduled Double Stage LTR reconstructive surgery. Ryan and I still went to work, and Beckett remained at home with his regular day nurse whom we had finally gotten back after days and weeks of petitioning with our insurance company for nursing hours. We had finally secured a nurse who, while she was a little quirky—like she used all my paper towels every day—was reliable and followed direction, and best of all, she took really good care of Beckett. Her name was Carol.

As we approached the surgery date, my time was consumed with planning everything for going out East. With the double stage LTR, Beckett would have surgery and remain at the hospital inpatient for two weeks, but then we would have to stay in the Philadelphia area for another four to six weeks as they would perform a weekly bronchoscopy on Beckett to look at the transplanted tissue in his airway and ensure it was healing correctly. So, we needed to plan for six to ten weeks out East. We decided to fly into Baltimore again and booked a long-term rental car for the entire time we would be there. Accommodation-wise, we would stay the first few nights after arrival and surgery at a nearby hotel and then would stay in the Ronald McDonald House and finally with some family friends in Delaware. I would take another leave from my job, and while Ryan would take a little time off, too, he would need to continue working (someone had to pay the bills) and just travel back and forth form his worksite to Philadelphia. My mom graciously agreed to come with us. Knowing that Ryan would have to come and go some, having another adult to help me was such a relief. In addition to planning things for Philadelphia, I also had to get things in order at home. We needed someone to check on the house, mow the yard, take care of Gus, our dog. What would we do with our mail? Our license plates needed renewing, and we needed the flu vaccine and dental cleaning appointments. There was so much to plan for and so much to do.

And yet, I found as the days narrowed until the time we would leave for Philadelphia leading us to take our first step towards a healthy airway for Beckett, all I wanted to do was pack Beckett in the car and drive West and not East, away from all the hospitals, all the pain he was soon to endure, away from the loss of time we would experience in recovery and inside of those hospital walls. I was scared—no, actually I was terrified. So many potential outcomes, hopefully only good, but there were always risks and the possibility that the surgery could fail, that his body would reject the transplanted tissue in his airway, or an infection could jeopardize the entire surgery. On days when fear seemed to drive my every move, I would snuggle Beckett in my arms and remind myself how far he had come and all that he had already overcome. And while the surgery was a big and scary one, we had done our research. We were in the right place. We had the right doctor and care team, and Beckett was ready. Most of all, I reminded myself that Beckett deserved this opportunity to get an airway that would allow him to live life to the fullest, to do all the things he couldn't do now. We were on the right road now; just taking that first step was hard and scary.

KEEPING OUR PACE

Double Stage Laryngotracheal Reconstruction (LTR)

On Thursday, October 4th, 2012, we woke in the city of brotherly love before the sun had risen. We packed our bags and tried to sneak bites of breakfast and sips of coffee when Beckett wasn't watching since he wasn't allowed to eat or drink anything before surgery. We loaded ourselves and the things we would need for the next twenty-four hours into our rental car and made our way to the entrance of the underground parking garage at the Wood Center of the Children's Hospital of Philadelphia, slipping below before the first ray of sunlight lit the sky. We went through the usual process of surgery check-in, pre-surgery waiting, etc. I watched Beckett's expressions as we signed papers and changed him into his little surgery gown and socks. He was observant, but calm. I was worried he would remember this place, this process, the hospital gown, but if he did, he showed no fear of it, and that calmed me. Shortly before 7:00 a.m., we hugged and kissed Beckett as we placed him once again into the arms of the surgery nurse and watched them walk away through the now somewhat infamous double doors leading to the operating room.

From there, we packed our things in the pre-surgery waiting room and moved across the hallway to the surgery waiting room. The receptionist there was the same one who had been there with each trip to the operating room at CHOP, and by now, she had started to recognize us. We met up with my mom and found a place to sit while we waited. Dr. Jacobs would first perform a bronchoscopy and, assuming everything looked good, would proceed with the double stage LTR surgery. We received word that everything looked great, and so began one of the longest waiting periods of my life. Surgery would take anywhere from six to eight hours in length. Dr. Jacobs would make a horizontal incision in Beckett's neck above his trach to access the damaged portion of the airway. After opening the windpipe, Dr. Jacobs would determine what size cartilage graphs would be needed. Once known, they would harvest the graphs from Beckett's right ribs. For the posterior graph, which will be on the back side of Beckett's airway, placement will take approximately two hours to secure into place. Then a silicone stent would be placed in the airway and secured with sutures. This would help hold the new tissues in place and keep the airway open. Next the anterior graft would be placed in the front of the airway. Approximate placement time was one hour. From there, Beckett would be sutured up and moved from the operating room to the Pediatric intensive care unit (PICU) where he would remain inpatient for the next two weeks.

In the waiting room, we busied ourselves working or reading or taking turns going to the cafeteria for some food or something to drink. Finally, at about 3:00 p.m., we received an update from Dr. Jacobs that surgery had gone very well. Both grafts had been placed, and Beckett had done just fine. He was being transferred from surgery to the PICU as we spoke, and once we finished with Dr. Jacobs, we were taken to his PICU room. In the PICU, Beckett would remain somewhat medically sedated for a while. He would be fed by an NG tube (feeding tube through the nose) for the next one to two weeks. After one week, Beckett would return to the OR to have the stent placed in his airway removed and a bronchoscopy done to look at the newly transplanted tissue. Hopefully, after two weeks, we would be discharged from the hospital assuming everything was healing as expected.

My least favorite part of the surgery and being placed in the PICU was the first thirty minutes after arriving into the unit. It's just crazy. The operating room care team is transitioning to the PICU care team, so there's a review of the case and medical stats, medications, treatments plans, etc. And usually other care teams are present; in our case it was the ENT care team. The number of doctors and nurses and other staff who were all in the room, trying to talk to us, provide us with updates and mess with Beckett was very overwhelming. Honestly, at that moment, all you want to do is see your baby and make sure they are as okay as possible. And sometimes you just want it all to stop. I remember, shortly after arriving at the PICU, the radiologist techs came to get another chest X-ray of Beckett as they wanted to validate everything was still in the right place after the transfer up from the operating room to the PICU. They gently slid the X-ray board under Beckett, but it was still enough movement to send Beckett into a pain fit of looking like he was crying and putting his hands up. The techs wanted to continue, but I intervened and said, "Just give him a minute." After being inpatient for so long and going through so many surgeries, I had found my voice and knew when to advocate for Beckett.

The remainder of the day, Beckett was calm with the occasional pain fit. He was on a fentanyl drip and would continue that during the night. They also added in rectal Tylenol to try to help him with the pain. The plan for the next twenty-four hours would be to continue to keep Beckett calm. Remember we had to keep his pain down, which would keep him from moving much initially to allow that new tissue to start to heal in its place. The next day, we were hopeful that the pain would start to subside enough to start feeds through his feeding tube in his nose and hopefully start weaning off the ventilator.

The following entries are from a journal I kept during Beckett's medical journey. These entries are for the most part verbatim from that journal. They describe in detail Beckett's recovery in the ICU and thereafter as well as my own physical and emotion state as I nursed him back to health.

Recovery Post Operation Day 1, written on Saturday, October 6th, 2012:

Yesterday, Beckett and my day started very early, which always happens when you are inpatient. It started at about 4:00 a.m. when the nurse and the respiratory therapist (RT) came in to do their assessments, and then the radiology tech at 5:00 a.m. for another chest X-ray. Next was the phlebotomist to take a lab draw for a CBC, just to ensure Beckett wasn't showing any signs of infection. And then the ENT team came and changed the gauze on Beckett's neck where the reconstruction took place and finally the surgical team to check the surgical site where the rib grafts were harvested. By 6:30 a.m., we had seen everyone except for the PICU team. The good news about yesterday was that Beckett was able to make some progress in his recovery. After the rounds in the morning, we stopped his fentanyl drip and allowed him to become more awake. He was still pretty sore, so once the meds had worn off, he wasn't his normal physically active self, but I could tell he was more alert mentally. By midmorning, he was removed from the ventilator but kept on half a liter of oxygen to help with his oxygen saturation rates. We also were able to start feeds by feeding tube and, by about midnight last night, had worked up to full feeds (50 ml per hour). Beckett's feeds will run constantly, twenty-four hours a day. Throughout the day yesterday we were able to manage Beckett's pain with just Tylenol every four hours, although they said that he could have morphine if needed. But like the trooper he always is, he was good on the Tylenol. This was good as it would help his bowels "stay awake." Last night we did give him a dose of morphine and then switched to oxycontin, which we gave every four hours (8:00 p.m., 12:00 a.m. and 4:00 a.m.). He was definitely much more comfortable last night and seemed to have slept well. All in all, it was a good day, and we are hopefully for another good one today.

Recovery Post Operation Days 2 & 3, written on Sunday October 7th, 2012:

Yesterday was a rougher day for Beckett, which isn't uncommon after surgery. Sometimes patients will get worse before they start to get better after an operation, especially a big one like Beckett had. He seemed to be in more pain and had a bad afternoon with his IVs. The IV in his foot (an extremely bad place for a twenty-one-month-old to have an IV) wouldn't flush, so they had to take it out. This, my friends, was a battle: Beckett vs. the nurse, Ryan, my Mom and me. Beckett is *so* strong, and so it took all of us holding him down before the mission was accomplished. Then because of Beckett thrashing and fighting against us, the IV in his arm became dislodged—great. Here we go again. So we had to remove that IV. Now, the IV's coming out might actually have been a good thing, because who likes to have an IV in, except that Beckett was placed prophylactically on a seventy-four-hour course of two antibiotics that had to be given via IV. *Dang!* Thank goodness our nurse knew to bring in the A-team for round two, so she called Mimi. Mimi was a salt-and-pepper-haired Asian woman from the IV team. She was very meticulous in her set-up and instructed each and every one of us on what we should be doing. It reminded me of my grandpa Kist, who practiced medicine as an oral surgeon. We all sat observing her and honestly stressing about the next session of trying to hold Beckett down and keeping him still enough to get the new IV in place. Thankfully, Mimi broke the silence and tension with her witty comments about Beckett's observation of her and if he was going to help her with the process. It's funny how the bedside manners of those caring for Beckett could make or break a difficult moment. And let me tell you, there is a reason Mimi is on the IV team. Her execution was flawless, and in no time and only a few tears, we had another IV up and running. Other than the increased pain and IV debacle, yesterday was just yesterday. The ENT group said the incision site in Beckett's neck still looked good and there were really no changes in orders from the PICU team. Last night started out very smoothly. I actually didn't have to get out of my bed in Beckett's room with him until about 3:00 a.m. The nurse was able to do what she needed to do and kept him sleeping, but at around 3:00 a.m., that all changed. Beckett was pissed, very pissed. I thought we had gotten him calmed down, and so went to use the bathroom in his room. I came back and he had puked in his bed with the nurse. We had just gotten him all cleaned up, bed cleaned, etc., and then more puke came up. By this point, I was on the verge of panic. One thing you *don't* want after them operating on your airway and "opening it up" was puke! The risk of aspiration and that aspiration in turn damaging the reconstruction was huge. So, I picked up Beckett out of his bed and just held him. I just wanted him calm, no more crying, oxygen desaturations and no more puke! I finally calmed him and told the nurse no more feeds, no more meds . . . nothing until the ENT doctors come to see him in the morning. So that was what we did. Of course, the one morning we wanted ENT to come at the butt crack of dawn they lollygag in around 8:00 a.m., but whatever, I was still happy they were finally there. I told them of the puke incidents, and they took a look and listen at Beckett. They thought he looked fine and were confident that the vomiting didn't compromise the reconstruction. *Thank* God! They also removed the drain, which was literally just a piece of a rubber band, in Beckett's neck at the incision site. Seriously, they used a piece of rubber band for the drain . . . Medicine is funny sometimes, isn't it? The rest of the morning Beckett has been relatively happy. We've been able to manage his pain using only Tylenol thus far today, and he is starting to smile and act like his normal silly self. His main and serious issue now is that he needs to poop! Poor thing has such a belly ache, and his constipation is being made worse with the pain meds and antibiotics. We did give him a suppository earlier, and we are hoping that will do the trick; if not, another med will be given to help. They just came for rounds and no big changes. We thought Beckett might be moved from the PICU to a surgery floor, but since he has a stent in his airway, he will remain in the PICU until Friday when he goes back to the operating room.

Recovery Post Operation Days 4 & 5, written on Tuesday, October 9th, 2012:

Yesterday was post-op day # 4 for Beckett. It was both an uneventful day and an eventful day. The morning started with the ENT team coming by. They thought Beckett's incision site in his neck looked great and was healing well. During the rounds, there were no changes except that, if Beckett didn't have a bowel movement today, an enema would be given. *Yikes.* Before going that route, we tried another glycerin suppository and more MiraLAX. Beckett took a good nap in the morning and woke up around lunch time. All morning we waited for Beckett to pass stool, but nothing. Finally, at about 2:00 p.m., Beckett had a serious stool. Unfortunately, it was while he was sitting on my mom's lap. I think the hospital is making both my mom and me crazy because, even though there was crap everywhere, literally, we were laughing so hard about the entire ordeal. We were honestly just *so* happy Beckett finally passed stool. So, after a change in pants for my mom and getting B somewhat cleaned up, we decided a bath was definitely in Beckett's future.

The remainder of the afternoon was spent by trying to keep Beckett entertained and changing more poopy diapers. Unfortunately, it was feast or famine with the stools. First, he couldn't go, and now he can't stop going! In the entertainment department, we are running out of tricks. We brought lots of toys, but those are getting old, as is the Disney channel and Sprout TV. Thankfully, yesterday, Beckett received a package at the hospital that contained some new Dalmatian slippers and a stuffed Dalmatian. It was definitely the highlight of his day!

Last night Beckett did not sleep well. His stomach was still churning from all the action in his belly, so he woke up almost every hour crying, I'm sure from stomach cramps. During the rounds this morning, no changes were made, and ENT also said things looked good. So, I am sure that it will just be another day of trying to entertain Beckett and hopefully getting some sleep. In other updates, it's been rainy here in Philadelphia for a couple of days now. Beckett has a window in his room, but it only looks out to the rooftop of another building that is part of the hospital. The days seem to be getting longer, and my energy levels are quickly diminishing. I've been at the hospital since surgery: five nights and starting day seven today. After more than a few days and nights here, you definitely feel like the walls around you are starting to close in on you. I am remaining hopefully that today and tomorrow will go by quickly and that Friday morning will be here before we know it. Once the stent is removed, Beckett will probably be returned to the ICU, but hopefully just for a night or two. Saturday he will be seen by Speech and Feeding. We are hoping that Beckett can take to oral feeds with his new airway just fine so that we can get out of here sooner rather than later. But if he shows any signs of aspiration or choking, we will likely remain inpatient longer.

Recovery Post Operation Day 6, written on Thursday, October 11th, 2012:

Up until today, I felt like I was in a mental fog from lack of sleep. Two nights ago, I decided instead of getting out of bed every hour to suction and calm B, it would be a good idea just to sleep in his crib with him. I actually did feel like I slept better, but my body is paying for it. Not only was I folded up like a pretzel to fit into the crib and lay around Beckett and all his wires and tubes, but also the mattress (if you can call it that) is only about four inches thick and probably not made for people over 40 lbs. Last night proved to be a much better night and I think the first night I have been able to sleep more than two hours straight in over a week. I was still up quite a bit, but at least it wasn't every hour as it has been for a while. Beckett continues to do well. There really haven't been any changes in the past couple of days; we've just been trying to pass the time. I was *so* bummed on Tuesday as I went through half of the day thinking it was Wednesday only to find out it was actually Tuesday. I seriously feel like I am living through the movie "Groundhog Day" with Bill Murry, where every day is the same day over and over. Thanks goodness today is Thursday, and tomorrow morning Beckett will be headed back to the OR to have his stent removed. We won't know what time he will go to surgery until tomorrow morning, but I am elated we are only about twenty-four hours away. Beckett is really starting to get back to his usual silly self. On Tuesday afternoon, we were allowed to start going for wagon rides around the unit. Beckett absolutely *loves* them being able to get out of his bed and check out some new scenery. By Wednesday morning, the staff started to refer to Beckett as "The Mayor" of the seventh floor PICU, as he waves at everyone when we go for walks. In addition, Beckett has made a new friend named Patrick. Patrick is the child life specialist who has been bringing Beckett new donated toys to play with each day. *Thank goodness!* It's really nice, and all the toys are brand new (so we don't have to worry about germs). So, if you have ever donated toys to a children's hospital, *thank you*! I can tell you firsthand that they make a world of difference to sick children.

Recovery Post Operation Days 7 & 8, written on Saturday, October 13th, 2012:

Beckett's trip to the OR yesterday went smoothly. The procedure only took about forty-five minutes, and they were able to successfully remove the stent. Once removed, the doctor advised that everything looked as he would expect one-week post-surgery. The doctor advised that he would perform another bronchoscopy on Beckett again next Friday and said that, if Beckett's airway reconstruction would show any signs of collapse or issues, those would likely become evident in this next week.

After the OR, Beckett was returned to the ICU. He slept for a good while, but then upon waking was back to his usual self. He is so incredibly resilient; it amazes me! The remainder of the afternoon was spent just hanging out in the room. No tours for the Mayor yesterday.

Last night, Beckett slept the best that he has since his first surgery. Of course, last night I couldn't sleep; that's always how it seems to work. This morning at 10:00 a.m., speech/feeding came to evaluate Beckett. We started with some strawberry yogurt, and at first, he wasn't sure, but then—you would have thought it was crack—he was loving it. Next was Cheerios; again, he loved it and did very well. No choking, gagging, just his usual eating self. Next, we tried milk. I thought Beckett did his usual stuff; however, the therapist had some concerns and made the recommendation of allowing Beckett to eat soft solids and dissolvable solids and then have his milk go through his feeding tube. I wasn't having it. Beckett not only *loves* his milk, but he was doing just fine, no differently than prior to surgery. So, after some explaining and a nipple hunt in Central Supply for a slower flow nipple, Beckett is now allowed to drink his milk orally as well. I've learned well enough by now that you have to be an advocate for your child, especially in these situations where you know their baseline better than anyone else. Shortly after the therapist cleared us, Beckett was moved from the ICU to the surgery floor. So, the Mayor's new office is (4 South, Room 1). We really loved all the RNs and DRs in the ICU, but Beckett is now stable enough to allow someone who is in need of the room to have it (currently there is a wait for an ICU room at CHOP). They are *very* busy. And on the positive side, our new room had a better view from the window and should be much quieter, which will be much better.

The remainder of the afternoon was spent getting settled into our new room. The plan as of now is to allow Beckett to try to eat orally as much as he will. Whatever he doesn't take by mouth will be given by his feeding tube. Fingers crossed—if we can get Beckett to eat everything orally without issues, there is a chance we will be discharged before the next bronchoscopy. This would be ideal. We would all recover, sleep and thrive if we are able to walk and explore not just the inside, but get some fresh air too! Finally, an update on Ryan. He flew back to Philadelphia this past Thursday, but has spent the entire day today in bed at the Ronald McDonald House. He has a scratchy throat and is not feeling well. We cannot risk exposing Beckett to anything, but it stinks he came to see Beckett, but hasn't been able to. In addition, he has to return to KC tomorrow to go back to work Monday. Traveling for Beckett's care has been immensely difficult in many ways, but we know we are receiving the best possible care for Beckett, and that makes it all worth it.

Recovery Post Operation Days 9, 10 & 11, written on Tuesday, October 16th, 2012:

Since being moved to the surgery floor, things have been going very well for Beckett. We were moved to the surgery floor on Saturday afternoon. On Sunday, he continued to take all his food orally. The highlight of our day on Sunday was that Bridget, the therapy dog, came to Beckett's room to visit. Beckett was *so* excited and thought Bridget was pretty funny!

Also, on Saturday afternoon, we took the Mayor on a couple of wagon rides. Since the stent is no longer in Beckett's airway, we were allowed a bit more freedom, so we went to the main lobby of the hospital and even snuck Beckett outside for a few minutes to get some fresh air.

Sunday night was a very good night for Beckett and finally for me too! Beckett slept from about 9:00 p.m. until 4:00 a.m. without any interruptions. I did the same, which is good. Saturday night I had a headache that wasn't going away, and by Sunday night, I thought if I don't sleep tonight, I am not going to last much longer; I felt like my body was starting to shut down on me from lack of sleep. Sunday morning, the ENT team came for rounds and said they would pull Beckett's feeding tube from his nose since he was eating everything orally. Originally, the nurse practitioner said something about staying in the hospital until Friday and the next bronchoscopy. I said, "No. Dr. Jacobs said we could leave once Beckett was eating everything orally and stable otherwise." She said she would have to check with him and would be back in a bit to pull his tube. About thirty minutes later, she was back. She pulled the tube, and we were discharged from the hospital. I was so thrilled and so thankful. I knew I was nearing the end of my ability to stay at the hospital day and night with Beckett; my body was refusing. So, in a tizzy, we started packing everything up. Thankfully, my aunt from Des Moines, was visiting Virginia for the weekend and came to CHOP to visit Beckett before catching her flight back. She was able to help my mom pack everything up at the Ronald McDonald House and gave me a ride to the airport to pick up a rental car. Finally, about noon, we were on the road with Beckett to Bear, Delaware. My parents used to live in Bear, Delaware, about six years ago, and thankfully for us, they have some amazing neighbors who offered to let us stay at their house with Beckett while he was here for treatment. So yesterday, we arrived at Peggy and Dave's and quickly settled in. You can just tell Beckett is thrilled to have more freedom and be able to go outside. And many of the neighbors here have loaned Beckett toys, so he thinks it's like Christmas with all the new toys here!

Recovery 15-days Post Operation:

On Friday, October 19th, 2012, Beckett went back to CHOP for his second bronchoscopy since the stent was removed. Dr. Jacobs said everything looked normal for two weeks post-op. The tissues were not totally healed yet, and there was still a bit of swelling in the airway, which is normal from surgery. He also slightly dilated Beckett's airway using a small "balloon." Thankfully, we were able to avoid being admitted to CHOP and returned back to Delaware after the procedure. The plan Dr. Jacobs advised at this time was that he wanted to perform another bronchoscopy on Beckett again this Friday (10/26/12), then again on (11/2/12) and again on (11/16/12). We knew we were here for the long haul but were hoping maybe we could return home around the 16th. Now it's looking like maybe the following week . . . Hopefully, we will be home by Thanksgiving. While we know this is the right course of action and want to stay until Beckett is cleared, it's hard to have patience. Like all things with Beckett, all we've ever needed, and still need, is time, time to grow and now time to heal. While our expectations were set as such, it's hard being away from home and, this week in particular, away from Ryan. He returned back to KC last Sunday (10/14) and won't be returning to Philadelphia until this coming Thursday (10/25). The 17th was our third wedding anniversary, but of course, we spent it miles apart. I think we are both ready for the day when we can celebrate birthdays and anniversaries together and not in hospitals, which has been the trend now for the past two years. Hopefully, time will pass quickly, and Beckett will continue to heal and stay healthy so we can return home and get life back to normal.

Recovery 22-days Post Operation:

On Friday, October 26th, 2012, we headed back to CHOP for Beckett's fourth bronchoscopy since his double stage LTR surgery. I thought our OR arrival time would be around 11:00 a.m., but much to my surprise, it was 7:15 a.m. The good news with being early is that it's less time Beckett has to wait to eat and usually the OR is more on time in the morning. The downside was that we would have to leave the house in Delaware at 5:30 a.m.! We arrived at CHOP at about 6:20 a.m., a little earlier than needed, but you never know how traffic will be around here. We checked into the pre-operative area and waited. Much to our surprise, we were called back to the pre-op room at 6:45 a.m. Perfect—I thought Beckett will be able to go early. Well, getting into the room early must have been a curse because Beckett didn't end up going back until 10:45 a.m.! Yikes! He was so bored and tired of being in the pre-op room, he ended up falling asleep in my arms, which wasn't a bad thing because the OR nurse just carried him back sleeping into the OR. About thirty minutes later, Dr. Jacobs came out to talk to Ryan and me in the waiting room. He said Beckett's airway looked great! Much less swelling than last week and no evidence of collapse. He also said there appeared to be no sign of infection, and the tissues appeared to be healed over. While a good report indeed, he advised that he still wanted to perform another bronchoscopy on Beckett again next Friday. "Cautious observation," he said. Shortly thereafter, we were on our way back to Delaware.

So back to the OR Beckett will go on November 2nd, 2012. Poor guy! He has just about had it with the hospital. As soon as we wheel his stroller into the pre-op area, the look on his face is like "Please, no!" It's heartbreaking. Hopefully, next week's report will be just as good and only one or two more bronchoscopies will be needed. This weekend, it's been nice to have Ryan here. This morning we went to Costco, Walmart and got some gas in the car. Everyone around here, including us, is preparing for Hurricane Sandy, aka "Frankenstorm." There is the chance that it will directly hit near Wilmington, Delaware, which is only about fifteen or so miles from here. So, we've stocked up on food, water, flashlights as well as diapers and milk for Beckett. Thankfully, Peggy and Dave are very prepared, too. They have a back-up generator and spent the morning securing deck furniture and other items outside. We are hoping it will turn out to sea or at least doesn't directly hit near us, but in the case that it does, we will be prepared.

Recovery 29-days Post Operation:

Beckett's bronchoscopy on November 2nd, 2012, went great! The doctor said that his airway looks perfect! The tissues appear to be completely healed over, and the majority of the swelling has subsided. *Yahoo!* I was hopeful maybe he would say go ahead and go home (since B had such a good report), but to be safe, he wants to take one more look at B's airway on November 16th, so we are here to stay for another two weeks.

From where we were when we started this journey over a month ago, the next two weeks should seem like a breeze, but both my mom and I are tired. And while we are extremely grateful that Beckett is doing so well and that we have such a nice place to stay, there really is no place like home. I am sure that I could list about a million things about home that I miss: my bed, our dog Gus, B's playroom in the basement, etc., but I think what I am missing the most is a sense of normalcy. I just want things to be back to normal, back to our routine, which doesn't involve a weekly trip to the OR. But for now, we are here to stay on the East Coast.

Editor's Notes:

It should be noted that, during our time with Beckett in Delaware while we waited for his airway to heal, was a time of great caution as we were very careful to keep Beckett away from others and isolated from any potential exposure to germs or a cold that could be devastating to his reconstructed airway. We did do outings, but kept them to outdoor places, and you can bet we were the people looking like germaphobes wiping down playground equipment or Lysol spraying the slides. I cannot stress this enough for other patients whose might be going through a similar surgery. As hard as it is to live in a bubble and miss out on things, protecting Beckett from getting sick was one of the number one reasons his LTR surgery was as successful as it was.

Recovery 43-days Post Operation:

On November 16th, 2012, our wheels hit the pavement on I-95 towards Philadelphia for Beckett's final bronchoscopy. His arrival time was 6:45 a.m. and luckily was taken back to the OR about 9:20 a.m. Dr. Jacob said Beckett's airway looked good, but there was a bit more swelling than two weeks ago. He probably would have dilated his airway, but then that would require another bronchoscopy in a week, so no action was taken. He advised that he wants to perform another bronchoscopy on Beckett again in January 2013, which stinks as we were hoping to not make another trip out here until March or maybe even May, but we need to do what's right for Beckett. Ryan and I are planning to set up a call with Dr. Jacobs in a few weeks just to have a better understanding of what the next six to twelve months would look like for Beckett. We have learned a lot about Beckett's airway in the past six weeks since reconstruction. We now believe that Beckett will likely be three or potentially even four years old before the trach will be removed due to his tracheomalacia (floppy airway). The tracheomalacia is just from being born prematurely, and there is no treatment. Beckett just needs to grow out of it. We also know that Beckett has a little bit of collapse right at his trach site, which may require surgical correction. We are hoping that the collapse will become less severe with growth. Tomorrow morning, we leave to *finally* return home. I feel like we've been here *forever* . . . so long I feel like I am forgetting little details about home. Our time here on the East Coast has been full of blessings: overall smooth and thus far successful for Beckett, sightseeing on the East Coast, many laughs with my mom, wonderful accommodations and company in Delaware. We have so much to be thankful for. Finally, with part of Beckett's airway rebuilt and more open, we've been able to start using the speaking valve more for short periods of time. He cannot tolerate it long-term due to the tracheomalacia, but it's still been so much fun to hear his voice and watch his own facial expressions as he hears himself for the first time and figures out the sounds he can make.

*End of journal entries

No place like home

As we arrived back in Kansas City, we fell back into our old routine. I started going back to work, which seemed strange after being gone for sixty days for Beckett's surgery, and thankfully our insurance reallocated nursing hours for Beckett's care while I was at work. And the best news was that we were able to get Carole back, who had cared for Beckett before. She had her quirks, but she was honest, dependable and really did give Beckett good care, so we were happy.

Shortly after returning to Kansas City, I received a call from Dr. Jacobs who said he was reviewing Beckett's last scope he had performed before leaving Philadelphia, and based on the swelling, he said he wanted to scope Beckett again in December of 2012. I remember upon hanging up I had a good long cry. Obviously, this was the right step, but honestly the thought of returning to Philadelphia after not even being home for one month was too much. Just the thought of trying to logistically plan everything again and traveling during the cold and flu season felt impossible. December 28th, 2012 was Beckett's operating room date. Thankfully, that gave us a little more time at home, and we could get through the holidays before heading back to CHOP.

In late November of 2012, the inevitable happened, and Beckett woke with a 102° temperature and vomiting. We were actually in Iowa at the time visiting family, and I remember feeling a strong urgency to get back home. My greatest fear with Beckett has always been readmission into the hospital. And if that was going to happen, my God it was going to happen close to home if I could help it. After all, I had just spent sixty days away from home. We made it back to Kansas City and thankfully were able to keep him at home with supplemental oxygen. I called CHOP to inform Dr. Jacobs that Beckett was ill, and I was terrified he would tell us the surgery was likely compromised. Thankfully, though, he said that, since the tissues had healed over, it should all be okay, but would still be a good idea to keep him healthy if we could.

It ended up taking Beckett almost three weeks, a course of antibiotics, breathing treatments and supplemental oxygen to finally get over his viral cold. Not to mention lots of sleepless nights and days of worry for me. Again, this was always my greatest fear with Beckett: something small, a cold, could take us off our relatively smooth path towards our destination and place us on a rocky road miles back from where we were. And was why I walked a tight rope when it came to visitors and taking Beckett places—I would do anything to keep him healthy and safe.

On Thursday, December 27th, 2012, we boarded a plane with Beckett for his fourth flight to the East Coast. It was nice that we had been in Saint Louis with my parents for Christmas, because there was a direct flight from Saint Louis to Philadelphia, so we didn't have to fly into Baltimore and then drive two-and-a-half hours like we had been when flying out of Kansas City. The flight was slightly delayed and a little crazy with all the holiday travelers. Thankfully, armed with some travel Lysol spray, Clorox wipes and a mask for B, we made it to Philadelphia without catching any bugs.

We made our way to the hotel and fed Beckett before venturing out to get some dinner. This time, we were staying near the airport and there was not a lot around, so we ended up eating at a Wawa's gas station. Sounds nasty, and I was skeptical, but they actually had a really nice and fresh deli inside. So good, in fact, we ate again for lunch the next day. Like the million times before, I called the CHOP surgery line to obtain our OR arrival time for the next day. Our arrival time was 6:30 a.m. An early morning it would be, but always better that way. We arrived at CHOP and checked in just before 6:30 a.m. We were called back within five minutes to the pre-operation room where we hung out until about 8:30 a.m. when Beckett was finally taken back to the OR. While we were waiting, Dr. Jacobs stopped by to see how Beckett was and chat with us before the scope. I was shocked when he came in and placed a red plug on Beckett's trach, in essence requiring Beckett to breathe solely through his airway and not his trach. Both Ryan and I were shocked that Beckett did as well as he did. He probably lasted a good two to three minutes (which felt like ten to me) before I asked Dr. Jacobs if we could remove the cap. He thought Beckett did surprisingly well with the capping test. Thereafter, an Respiratory Therapist came and tested Beckett's airway pressures when using the speaking valve to see how well he was tolerating it. Of course, his performance left much to be desired, as he was not happy when someone with scrubs entered his room (i.e., anyone at this moment in this setting), which in turn impacted his ability to breathe calmly when he was crying. But in the end, we ended up getting the green light to start using the speaking valve up to thirty minutes twice a day. I was so excited! It felt like a huge jump instead of the tiptoe steps we had been taking for the past nearly two years.

After a visit from the pre-operation nurse, a quick exam from the surgery nurse practitioner, and a chat with the anesthesiologist, Beckett was finally ready to go. Now normally Beckett was good if one of the operating room nurses just carried him into the operating room. Well, my friends, after October and all the recurring trips to the operating room, Beckett wasn't falling for that anymore. CHOP did offer a pre-med aka "giggle juice" that they would give to help kids relax and not be stressed going into surgery, but we tried that in April of 2012 and Beckett came out of anesthesia like an angry bull, so since that experience, we didn't like to give it to him. And so, that day, I took Beckett back to the operating room myself. That's right—the doctors and nurses advised I could carry him myself to the operating room. So that's what we did. I was out-fitted in scrubs from head to toe including a real cute surgery bonnet to complete my look and the protocols. It was very interesting to walk the long hallways that we normally just watched Beckett disappear down and to enter the operating room where the procedure would take place. Beckett was no fool and I could tell he was still on edge about where we were headed, but I believe the fact that I was holding him made him feel safer. Once in the OR, I held Beckett in my arms while the anesthesiologist administered gas through his trach to put him to sleep. Once he turned into a wet noodle in my arms, I placed him on the table and kissed him good-bye. It was a little eerie as his eyes were still open, but I wasn't afraid or sad. I knew he was in good hands, and unfortunately after sending your baby off to the operating room more times than you can count, you become numb to these kinds of things.

I went back to the pre-op area, met Ryan and we checked into the surgery waiting room with Theresa, the waiting room secretary. You know that you have been coming to the hospital and operating room too much when the waiting room secretary knows your child's name and yours when you walk through the door, as does half the pre-op and post-op staff. We only had to wait about thirty minutes before being called to one of the consultation rooms to meet Dr. Jacobs. He came into the room and advised that he was very pleased with the scope and now would consider the LTR in October a success. Thank you, Lord! Here I was happy because we could start using the speaking valve, and now I was elated because we could finally declare the double stage LTR surgery a success. All the coordination of everything, the pain for Beckett, the sleepless nights in the hospital, the time on the East Coast, everything . . . it was all worth it because we were making progress. Big progress.

Dr. Jacobs advised that we didn't need to come back for another scope until May or June of 2013. Even better news! He did advise, again, that Beckett did have a pretty severe collapse right at his trach site, which would likely require another graph to correct, but that wouldn't happen for a number of months/years. We knew this coming out of the first surgery, so while a reminder that we would be traveling this road for a bit more time, not new news. And after all, nothing could be bad news after all the good news we were just fed.

Rebalancing

As the calendar turned to 2013, we kicked off the year by celebrating Beckett's golden birthday, turning two on January 2nd, 2013. Of course, Beckett's birthdays were never big to-dos with tons of little friends attending. Instead, it was celebrated with a low-key Mickey Mouse themed birthday at home in order to maintain his health and limit his germ exposure. His big gift was a fish tank from Ryan and I, which we knew Beckett would love as he always loved the fish tanks we saw during doctors' appointments and hospital visits.

January 2013 also brought big changes for me as I was nearing a breaking point in my personal/professional life and, after being at this point for quite some time, finally realized it was time that I needed to make a change as I could continue on this road no longer. Seeing that Beckett's medical needs weren't going to end anytime soon, I decided I needed to reevaluate my career. My dilemma was I had always been very career driven. Before Beckett, I would log more than sixty hours a week at work, and even when I wasn't working, I was reading or researching or something related to work. I worked hard, really hard, to get to where I was, and when I found out I was pregnant in 2010, I thought, *No big deal. I can do this. I am a woman who can do it all, babies, housework, career, etc.* Even shortly after Beckett arrived, I was still optimistic that I could still do it all. In fact, I can remember the day after I delivered him while still in the hospital I was on my computer and working on a monthly report. Crazy? Maybe, but at the time work was a sense of "normalcy" to the crazy world my life had become overnight. Still, with the prolonged hospital stays, my thought was, *Okay, we just need to get to this milestone (Beckett's due date, get Beckett off the ventilator, the next bronchoscopy) and then life will become more normal.* After twelve months of this balancing act, I was tired. I was spread thin. With Ryan traveling Monday through Thursday, I felt like a single mom. But not just a single mom, a single mom to a baby with lots of extra needs: therapy sessions, doctors' appointments and the stress of knowing at any moment Beckett could become critical due to the state of his airway. At night, I would pray that Beckett wouldn't pull his trach out or that it wouldn't plug, and if it did, I prayed I would hear his alarms and be able to save him. And every morning, I prayed for the strength to get through one more day. I was living day by day, at times minute by minute. It was all I could do to survive.

Ryan and I discussed me leaving my job a couple of times, but again I was hanging on. I really liked—no, loved my job. Yeah, there was a lot of stress and bullshit, but that's every job. I enjoyed what I was doing, but more than that, I had the best team: a team of coworkers and management who had not only seen me through everything, but also supported me. They gave me the sense of normalcy or maybe a good distraction for nine to ten hours a day. But twelve months of trying to be super mom and career woman had taken a toll on my personal happiness, my marriage, Beckett's development . . . pretty much all the things that were my everything. Outside of work, I was mean, disgruntled and short tempered. I was so exhausted I only had the energy to deal with work people's bullshit and patience for Beckett; anything outside of that, forget about it. Ryan and my relationship remained strained. Instead of giving him credit for working hard for our family and all he did, I focused on all his faults and what he wasn't doing. Every week was the same conversation and the same argument. And in August of 2012, when the speech therapist came to evaluate Beckett, he scored on the three-to-six-month level—Beckett was eighteen months old. Things were clearly falling apart, not so much at work, but at home.

In October of 2012, when Beckett had his LTR surgery, I took family medical leave act time at work and really disconnected for the first time since Beckett arrived. I had taken leave time when he was finally discharged from Children's Mercy in June 2011, but I still worked part time, so I never really got a break. This time, I totally checked out. My focus was solely Beckett and myself: his surgery, recovery and development and my personal healing from the mess of the previous twenty-two months. By the end of my leave, his surgery was declared a success, and in a recent assessment by the speech therapist, he tested out at eighteen to twenty-one months (he was now twenty-four months). And ultimately, I realized I could not continue at the pace I was. Something was going to break; either I was going to go loco, Ryan and I's marriage would completely crumble, or Beckett would get to kindergarten and be too far behind to start . . . or maybe all three.

And so, I made the decision to leave my job. I am sure some people are reading this and think I am crazy to see this as a "hard decision." They would love to leave their job if they were able. Don't get me wrong; I was very excited and blessed to be able to do so. The "hard" part for me was letting go. I was raised to *never* give up and, in a sense, I felt like I was giving up, like I couldn't do it all anymore . . . and for me, that was hard to swallow.

The plan was that I would stay on until April to train my backfill and allow a team member who was on leave to return. However, much to my surprise, shortly after my resignation I was offered a part-time position with my company, which I accepted. I felt so blessed to have the opportunity, not only to continue to contribute at work, but to better balance my life and meet the ongoing needs of Beckett. It's funny how sometimes pieces of life just fall into place. For the first time in a long time, that felt like the case for me.

As my work-life balance improved, so did things under our roof. I had more time to focus on Beckett's therapies, which at the time included lots of sign language and speech therapy. His tolerance of the speaking valve had continued to lengthen (hopefully an indication that he was growing out of his floppy airway), and we continued to work on sign language. At that point, Beckett could sign around seventeen signs, but he definitely understood more than he could sign or express and was able to identify the following: body parts, people (Mom; Dad; Gus, our dog; family; friends) and objects such as trees, TV and animals.

In terms of vocalization, Beckett could say "Mama" and "Dada." We were working to expand his vocalized words, but when the speaking valve was on, he still really liked to hear himself so we would usually just hear lots of babbling, just like you would hear from a baby who is experimenting with their voice. Overall, speech was moving right along, and based upon the progress we had been able to make with signs and vocalization, our speech therapist wasn't concerned about speech. It would come, once Beckett was mechanically able to vocalize more.

The greatest challenge for Beckett, and me, at that moment was trying to get him to eat more table food. It was something we had put off pushing him on as we needed him to have good nutrition for his surgeries and growth, and thus he had been sustained mostly with PediaSure and some table food. But he couldn't be sustained that like forever, so we needed to start getting him to eat more actual food instead of the dense nutrition drink of PediaSure.

We started by reducing his PediaSure intake and adding in whole milk. Then, we reduced the overall amount of milk he received in hopes to make him more hungry to eat table food. The first week was immensely challenging, and by Friday afternoon, I had a serious breakdown. I called the dietitian we had been working with, and we made some changes that helped, but there is nothing more frustrating than a child who will not eat. I think it was especially emotionally draining for me for a couple of reasons. For one, when Beckett received his tracheotomy in March of 2011, they also wanted to give him a feeding tube in his belly. Ryan and I decided against it as we wanted to give Beckett the opportunity to eat orally, but they told us if Beckett didn't eat or didn't gain weight, it might become medically necessary. So since then, I had always feared Beckett would need this if he didn't eat. And two, we were just waiting for Beckett to grow and his airway to get bigger so that we could complete his second airway surgery at which point the trach would be removed. So, if he didn't eat, he wouldn't grow . . . further delaying decannulation (trach removal).

Like all new changes that are hard at first, slowly and with deliberate focus, Beckett started to eat more table food. His diet, though, was terrible. He would hardly eat any fruits, vegetables or proteins. He had texture aversions as well as what they call a low-reg mouth, which basically meant he liked really flavorful foods. For example, he loved Pringles pickle-flavored chips. So, it was challenging to say the least, but like all things, we just needed time and patience.

As spring turned to summer, my new schedule gave me more time with Beckett and allowed us to do more things than we had ever done before. We took Beckett sledding for the first time, took a trip to my grandmother's house in Iowa for a week, met and played with our cousins in Saint Louis, played with neighborhood friends. Such simple things and yet things Beckett had been unable to do for the first two years of his life either because he was unable to or because we feared him getting exposed to germs. But those little tastes of freedom felt like a door opening from inside a dark room. Those first rays of light were so bright and inviting, and we were ready to walk out that door all together. However, we still had one more big surgery to get through before we could do that.

On June 12th, 2013, we made another trip back to CHOP for a visit with Beckett's team there. He was seen in the clinic on Thursday by Dr. Jacobs and the ENT team as well as Dr. Piccione, his pulmonologist. Then on Friday, Beckett was taken to the operating room for another bronchoscopy. Dr. Jacobs was wanting to see how the tissues from the double stage LTR were looking, as well as gauge Beckett's tracheomalacia (floppy airway) since his last bronchoscopy six months earlier. Ryan and I sat hopeful for good news as we always did. We thought maybe Beckett would be able to have his single stage LTR and have his trach removed in the fall of 2013, but most likely, it would end up being the spring of 2014.

I'll never forget the smile on Dr. Jacobs' face when he greeted us in one of the consultation rooms within the surgery waiting area. Dr. Jacobs advised that Beckett's airway looked great. He said that Beckett's airway had grown much over the past six months since his last scope in December, and not only did the grafts from the surgery last October looked great, the tracheomalacia (floppy airway), which was hindering trach removal, was gone. Dr. Jacobs went on to say that, based upon what he saw in the OR that day, Beckett would be a candidate for a single stage LTR (trach removal) in August or September of this year. I'm not sure Ryan and I could even process the words that he was saying fast enough to react. And I think we were both waiting for the "But . . ." and then the bad news to come at us like a stab in the chest, just like so many times before. But this time, the bad news never came. Instead, that door with the light shining through opened just a bit more, allowing us this time to stand in its warmth. *Sooner,* I thought, *sooner than later, we will be able to walk through that door.*

By the end of July 2013, we were in the final stages of planning our next big trip to Philadelphia for Beckett's single stage LTR surgery and trach removal. Friday, August 23rd, 2013, was the big day when Beckett would go to the OR, but the bigger travel plan would look like this: On Wednesday, August 21st, Ryan, Beckett, my mom and I would fly from Kansas City to Baltimore. From there, we would rent a car and drive to Philadelphia. Upon arrival to Philadelphia, we would check into a hotel where we would have to stay initially until we could see if we could get into the Ronald McDonald House. We were currently on the Ronald McDonald House's waiting list, as with limited space and lots of families needing housing, they were booked up. Obviously, all the travel expenses we had to pay out of pocket, with the hotel being the most expensive, so the Ronald McDonald House really helped us out when we could stay there. On Thursday, August 22nd, Beckett would have a couple of clinic appointments with ENT, pulmonology and pre-anesthesia. Then on Friday, August 23rd, Beckett would go to the operating room for his big and, what we hoped, his final airway surgery.

In terms of the surgery itself, Beckett would have a single stage LTR. It was basically the exact same surgery as Beckett had in October of 2012; the only difference was that they were only doing one rib graft placement and the trach would be removed during the procedure. Once the surgery was completed, Beckett would be placed in the ICU where he would remain intubated (breathing tube in) through his nose for anywhere between four to six days. The breathing tube would act as a stent and help ensure that the newly placed graft stayed in place and didn't collapse. During this time, he would be fed via a feeding tube (through the other nostril) and TPN (IV fluids) until he was extubated (breathing tube removed). Once the breathing tube could be removed and assuming his airway looked good, they would allow him to start trying to eat orally again. Once he was taking in enough for food orally, they would pull the feeding tube, and we would be discharged from the hospital. Total inpatient time was estimated to be anywhere from seven to fifteen days.

Then we would return to CHOP every Friday for trips to the operating room for Dr. Jacobs to perform bronchoscopies on Beckett's airway, just like the previous surgery. Dr. Jacobs would look at the graft and ensure it was healing and not showing any signs of potential infections, collapse, etc. We would continue the Friday trips to the operating room until the graft was healed over and Dr. Jacobs was comfortable with us heading back home.

As July turned to August, our focus was on making the necessary arrangements to be away from home for a long period of time again and keeping Beckett healthy. And by keeping Beckett healthy, we basically went back to living in a "lockdown" where we limited visitors, trips out of the house and became hand washing/sanitizing machines. It was hard to "stay in" given that it was summer and that was usually the time when we could actually get out of the house since it wasn't the cold, flu and RSV season, but would be worth the sacrifice to know there wouldn't be a setback in the surgery date because of an illness.

On August 12th, 2013, I took Beckett to some pre-surgery appointments we had set up at Children's Mercy in Kansas City for his surgery at CHOP. A blood draw, chest X-ray and ventilator clinic appointment with tracheal aspirate were all completed. By the end of our two-and-a-half-hour visit, I was exhausted from wrestling with Beckett, consoling him, drying tears and realizing just how much the coming weeks were going to suck. You would think round two would be easier than round one, but I actually thought it might be worse. I was wise to the nerves of surgery, pain of recovery, sleeplessness of our hospital stays and homesick of being away from home for so long. And you know what? So was Beckett. He was already starting to grow weary of parking garages, florescent lights, white coats and scrubs, but now he totally was. I was exhausted just thinking about the coming weeks with Beckett but tried again to focus on what needed to be done and getting those things completed. As I learned along this journey, just focus on the little things. Get those done, and they will add up to big things.

THE LAST PUSH

Single Stage Laryngeal Reconstruction (LTR)

On Wednesday, August 21st, 2013, my Mom, Beckett and I made it to Philadelphia after approximately eight hours of travel which included a flight from Kansas City to Baltimore and then the drive from Baltimore to Philadelphia. Minus the two-hundred-pounds of crap we had with us, a rental car that was originally too small to fit our two-hundred-pounds of crap, and traffic, the day went smoothly.

We settled into our hotel shortly after 3:00 p.m. and spent the afternoon going for short walks around the outside of the hotel. At two-and-a-half years old, Beckett was a busy toddler and one who needed to stretch his legs after sitting for hours of travel. I'll never forget a man exiting our hotel telling Beckett that he liked his necklace. What the hell? I could write an entire book on the odd comments and painful interactions I had with people and Beckett when he had a trach. Thankfully, though, at this point in our journey, my skin was thick, and I brushed off his comment and replied with my usual, "Thanks!"

Once settled and Beckett had walked off some energy, we spent the afternoon trying to figure out where we would be staying after Saturday. We had planned to stay at a hotel near the airport from Thursday until Saturday and then check into the Ronald McDonald House on Saturday until we were discharged from the hospital, but they could never guarantee us a room as once a family was checked in they didn't force them to leave if their child was still inpatient or undergoing care. All we could do was call each day and hope that a room was available. Needless to say, it made for a very stressful situation of trying to plan logistics and financials for our trip. Somehow, though, they called us at 2:00 p.m. and said they would have a room available starting Friday afternoon.

True to any stay with a toddler in a hotel, no one sleeps, and Thursday was another early morning of the last clinic appointments at CHOP before Beckett would go to the operating room on Friday. We met with ENT and pulmonology at 7:30 a.m. and 8:00 a.m. The appointments went well, and we surprised Dr. Jacobs, Rosemary, NP, and Dr. Piccione with one of the Beckett t-shirts we had made. In an effort to offset some of our travel expenses and to celebrate Beckett finally having his trach removed, I had shirts made that said, "Beckett's Decannulation Celebration . . . A New Adventure Starts Today." The care team was so excited they put their shirts on right away, and I will forever have etched in my mind a picture we took of me holding Beckett and Dr. Jacobs and Rosemary with their shirts on.

We spent the remainder of the afternoon grabbing forgotten items from the store and then resting. Beckett napped, and I tried to rest, also. I felt like I was about to head into a battle with Beckett's surgery and recovery. The first time had taught me so much, and I knew this time more than ever I needed to be rested and ready. Ryan arrived later that evening, as he had work commitments to wrap up before heading to Philadelphia. A call into the surgery hotline confirmed what we already knew: Beckett would be Dr. Jacobs' first case in the morning, and so we were to arrive at the pre-surgery area at 6:00 a.m.

I remember reflecting as I went to bed that this was the last day Beckett would have a trach, but like so many times along the journey with Beckett, I didn't allow myself to really believe it and relish in it, as a setback always seemed to come.

The sun rose on Friday, August 23rd, 2013, today was the day . . . decannulation day. We arrived at the pre-surgery area just after 6:00 a.m., got checked in and shortly thereafter were placed into a pre-surgery waiting room. Surprisingly, Beckett was very brave as we went through the same pre-surgery process we had gone through countless times before. And then, of course, we waited until it was time, the operating room was set and they were ready for Beckett.

I suited up in the "bunny suit" of scrubs once again and walked Beckett back to the operating room. The room itself is definitely an unmistakable place: bright lights, lots of equipment, shiny utensils, everyone in blue surgical suites with masks and surgical hats on. I don't blame him one bit for clinging to me and dropping big alligator tears off his cheeks onto my shirt. He was no fool. I held him close and sang "Mr. Moon" over and over until the gas hooked to his trach took over and I felt his body go limp in my arms. With the help of the nurses, I gently laid my sweet first born on the operating room table and kissed him goodbye. He was such a brave boy. And so, as with each surgery before, we proceeded to the waiting room where we would wait. They officially started at 8:00 a.m., and they said it would take anywhere from four to five hours to complete the surgery. Ryan and I would receive updates from the family nurse about every hour on how things were progressing and what they were doing at that moment. And once he was done, he would be moved from surgery to the ICU where we would be reunited with him. As the clock slowly ticked by and morning turned to afternoon, Ryan and I were starting to get concerned as surgery was lasting much longer than anticipated. But finally, at 2:30 p.m. (after six-and-a-half hours of surgery), he was done. Everything had gone just fine, and he was moved to his ICU room around 3:00 p.m.

Once the teams transitioned Beckett's care, we were finally able to see Beckett up close, hold his hands, cradle his head and talk to him. No one looks good coming out of surgery, but this time he looked rougher than before. He had an incision site and was bruised on his left chest from the rib graft harvest. In his right arm he had an IV and a PICC line (peripherally inserted central catheter) near his chest. A PICC line essentially gives access to the large central veins of the heart. For Beckett, the PICC line was a good thing, if you remember our IV debacle from his last surgery where Mimi had to come to the rescue. In general, PICC lines are more stable and allow the team to administer multiple meds intravenously. Beckett's neck was covered with a dressing that went all the way around his neck. We did peak underneath it with the nurse, and currently there was a drain sewn into the incision site on his neck. That should hopefully come out by Monday. In his right nostril was a breathing tube that was sutured in, and in his left was a feeding tube. In addition, he was hooked up to all the other tubes and wires that come with a stay in the ICU. Again, another picture etched in my mind and unfortunately a very sad one.

Since arriving in the ICU, Beckett had been kept pretty heavily sedated. However, the ideal state would be to have him awake but just kind of out of it. This was probably our biggest obstacle at the moment. We wanted Beckett to be comfortable and not in pain, but awake enough to keep up respiratory function and muscle movement. However, we didn't want him too awake so that he would try to pull out his breathing tube or any of the other lines and tubes currently attached to him. Later that evening, we started to wean Beckett off some of his pain meds, and every once in a while, he would try to open his eyes, which was usually followed by a grimace and tears. We could tell he was crying but couldn't with the breathing tube down. The plan for the first couple of days post operation was to try to find the right balance of medications that allowed Beckett to be comfortable, but also not overuse them. That evening, Ryan and my mom headed to the Ronald McDonald House, and I slept on the small vinyl-covered couch near the windows in Beckett's room. I felt like a huge elephant had been lifted from my chest upon the completion of Beckett's surgery and stable placement of him in the ICU. However, we were at no point of celebration. Like the single stage LTR, we had a long recovery road and lots more healing that needed to be done before we could declare his surgery a success and know that we had left his life with a trach behind for good.

The following entries are from a journal I kept during Beckett's medical journey. These entries are for the most part verbatim from that journal.

They describe in detail Beckett's recovery in the ICU and thereafter as well as my own physical and emotion state as I nursed him back to health.

Recovery Post Operation Day 1, "Fragile & Medicated," written on Saturday, August 24th, 2013:

Our first night post-op was a bit rough, but I would expect nothing less. Beckett was kept on continuous drips of fentanyl (painkiller) and dexmedetomidine (sedative), but they were relatively low doses. From about 9:00 p.m. until 12:00 a.m., the anesthesia from surgery wore off and he was waking in pain about every two hours. They would give him a "rescue" dose of fentanyl that would calm him and allow him to rest, but only for a short while. Around midnight, the drip dosages were increased, and rectal Tylenol was added. We had tried oral Tylenol through the feeding tube earlier in the day, but it made Beckett vomit. His poor belly is so empty, and he is so pumped up on meds I am sure he feels as if his insides are turning inside out. Finally, at about 12:30 a.m., he settled a bit more, but additional rescue doses were needed to get him through the night.

This morning after shift change, additional changes were made to the meds. In addition to the fentanyl (painkiller) and dexmedetomidine (sedative), they also added in Midazolam (form of valium for treating anxiety). This seemed to do the trick. But in addition to those three, he is also receiving the following via IV: two different antibiotics, Prevacid and IV fluids for hydration. I can honestly say, in all of Beckett's hospitalizations, he has never had these many "lines" and pumps going into him at one time.

ENT came this morning, and we changed Beckett's neck dressing. The incision site looks good, and there is minimal drainage, which is good. From a chest X-ray, it showed slight fluid buildup in Beckett's right upper lung and that the breathing tube was a little too deep in his airway. For the fluid, we've started percussion treatments to Beckett's chest, which is basically just lightly beating on his chest and back to loosen the fluid . . . You can imagine how much he loves that with a bruised and wounded rib cage. Then because the breathing tube is sutured in his nose and we cannot risk it coming out, ENT basically just un-taped the tube, put slight pressure on the stitches pulling it in an outward motion and then re-taped it. Beckett required a few "rescue" doses of pain meds during all of this. When the critical care team came for the rounds this morning, they kept his pain/sedative/anxiety medications as is since Beckett is finally comfortable but added in Zofran since Beckett vomited again this morning and also wrote orders to start feeds. Hopefully, this will help his poor belly feel better.

All in all, this recovery is night and day from the last one. The last time, Beckett was medicated but only for the first day really, and then he was awake and interactive. This time Beckett will remain very medicated until Wednesday of next week when he is tentatively scheduled to have the breathing tube pulled assuming all looks good on Tuesday when they take him back to the operating room for a bronchoscopy to examine the graft. Beckett is fragile in that the breathing tube is sutured in, but it can still move with Beckett's movement, which we do not want. Its purpose right now is to hold the rib graft in place, and with each movement we risk it moving in his airway. If Beckett rolls over or becomes too alert and pulled out the tube, it would be extremely detrimental to his recovery. Because of all this, we cannot pick up Beckett and hold him. We can just cradle him with our hands while he lays in his bed. It's so heartbreaking when he reaches for us and we cannot hold him.

In addition to the fragile breathing tube, Beckett is also at a higher risk of developing pneumonia since he is so sedentary. Thus, we are trying to "barrel roll" him or reposition him from side to side and on his back about every four hours to get some movement and break up any accumulating fluid in the lungs. Furthermore, we are having to wash Beckett's mouth out with a little sponge on a stick to help kill any bacteria that might be forming/growing in there that could lead to pneumonia, as well. So, we are in a whole different ballgame this time around. I'm not sure one is easier than the other as they are just both so different. But one thing that is the same and for sure is that the next bronchoscopy and tube removal cannot come soon enough.

Recovery Post Operation Day 2, "Poop & Paralysis," written on Sunday, August 25th, 2013:

Wow . . . well, the last twenty-four hours have definitely made me decide that the recovery last fall was *way* easier than our current recovery. Where to start . . . Let's start with the poop. No post-op recovery ever goes by without talking about the infamous, but always elusive, poop. We knew getting Beckett back stooling would be an issue. It's an issue at home, so given the added medications, especially the painkillers that slow mobility, we were in for a real challenge. So currently, Beckett has received just about *everything* to help him poop: prune and grape juice through his feeding tube, MiraLAX, glycerin suppositories, gas drops, Senokot, Colace and even a Fleet Enema! Still thus far, no poop (unbelievable!). Normally this wouldn't be such an issue except that Beckett's belly is *so* full of air (always seems to happen somehow in surgery) and now he is on continuous feeds (a pump is keeping a nutritional formula running into his belly 24/7), so things need to get moving. In addition, he is in pain that makes him awake from his meds and move his body in an unsafe manner, which brings me to our next topic of paralysis. As previously stated, we want Beckett comfortable and slightly sedated, but not so sedated that we can't bring him back off the meds by Wednesday when they pull the breathing tube as we need him awake enough to breathe on his own. He is still on a ventilator now and will remain so until Wednesday. Yesterday with the three medications that Beckett was on, we were still struggling to keep him comfortable, and as we went into last night, it only got worse. We now feel that Beckett's pain from the surgery is under control and that he is waking from the meds owing to stomach cramps from needing to poop/fart and from just being agitated with his situation. Therefore, last night, we gave him a medication to temporarily medically paralyze him (*scary*) and allow us to give him the enema. The thought was he would poop after the paralysis wore off and we would all have a peaceful night of sleep. Of course, this did not happen, and so as the night progressed, not only did Beckett not pass stool, but we continued to struggle to keep him in a safe state. He would wake and thrash his legs and arms and try to sit up. With the exception of 11:00 p.m. to 2:00 a.m. when we both managed to sleep, I would cautiously watch Beckett and the monitors for any signs that he was about to go crazy and then I would nearly lay my entire body over his to restrain him and keep him still until the nurse could administer a "rescue" dose of valium and painkiller. Talk about a stressful and exhausting experience. By morning, we had administered twenty-five "rescue" doses and increased the dosing on his continuous drips by double if not more. A "rescue" dose is where the nurse will basically administer an extra boost of the meds very quickly and hopefully calm Beckett back down quickly. I can remember between 2:00 a.m. and 3:00 a.m. talking with the NP concerned with how much we were increasing the drips and how many times we were having to "rescue" Beckett. Apparently, Beckett has quite a high tolerance to these meds. When the attending doctor came before the rounds this morning, I said, "We need a new plan." Another day/night like last night and I am pretty sure I would be needing the valium and other meds just as much as Beckett. And so we added two more narcotics to Beckett's current medicine IV concoction, but I am happy to announce for the first time since Friday, Beckett finally really rested today. We are still awaiting what will probably now be a massive blowout in his diaper but will probably have a party when it happens. Poop in the ICU is a big deal, people.

In other updates, Beckett's labs this morning looked good. His chest X-ray continued to show some compromise in his right upper lung so we made some slight adjustments on his ventilator settings, so that should help.

Recovery Post Operation Day 3, "No Poop & A Fever," written on Monday, August 26th, 2013:

Last night was a much better night. Both B and I slept, and he only required two rescues, one at 2:00 a.m. and another at 6:00 a.m. Today, his current medicine mixtures have again allowed him to rest, but not be too sedated. He will still wake occasionally, open his eyes, stretch, etc., but he is a much calmer man than a few days ago. And thus far today, no rescues. Here are the additional updates for the day:

- IVs/Access Ports: Last night, Beckett's IV in his arm blew so we had to put another in his foot. Thank goodness for the sedation, because he didn't even move through the entire event. His port in his arm, which is where all of his sedation and pain meds are given except rescues and the antibiotics, continues to look good and be functional.

- Wound sites: ENT came this morning and removed the drain from Beckett's neck. With the drain removal, they also stopped the antibiotics that Beckett was receiving. The incision site at Beckett's neck is sutured with dissoluble stitches as is the one on his chest where the rib graft was taken from.

- Poop: Or shall I say lack thereof. Poor baby. He seriously looks like a little Buddha man. His belly just continues to get bigger and bigger. So, today's action plan was we added in Lactulose. It's a stronger laxative given through his feeding tube. The attending also did a rectal exam (again, thank goodness for the sedative) to see if there was stool near the exit door. Unfortunately, there wasn't. So, we got an X-ray of his belly. There is basically just a ton of air in his belly. The good news is that from previous X-rays it's moving its way through the colon, but the bad news is it's not moving fast enough to bring Beckett much comfort. We have also started to use something called a red rubber. I'll spare you the details of what this fun thing does, but I am sure you can imagine.

- Lung collapse: The good news of the day, the atelectasis (collapse) in Beckett's right upper lung showed improvement today from previous days.

- Fever spike: The bad news of the day, Beckett spiked a temperature of 102° and had an elevated heart rate this morning. Fevers and elevated heart rates post-surgery aren't uncommon, but unfortunately, they are usually a sign of an infection. So, we ran a CBC (complete blood count) and another blood test this morning, as well as some blood cultures. The CBC and other blood tests came back within normal ranges, which is great. The cultures we have to wait to grow out a day or so before we know anything. Regardless, ENT wanted to continue Beckett's antibiotics for an additional twenty-four hours since he will go to the operating room tomorrow. The good news is that since the spike, a dose of Tylenol was given, and his temperature has remained within normal ranges.

And so, the plan for the coming days is as follows: Tomorrow, Beckett is on the operating room schedule for 1:30 p.m. They will remove his current breathing tube, perform a bronchoscopy on him and look at the graft and the insert another tube, but this time through his mouth. He will then return to the ICU. Assuming that all looks well, the plan will be to stop Beckett's sedation on Wednesday morning (Lord help us!) and allow him to wake up. When he is ready, ENT will pull his breathing tube in his room in the ICU. I am nervous, scared and excited for this moment. As I sat near his bedside last night watching him sleep, I felt a sense of irony about his current state. Here we are ending our journey with a trach just as it stated, with an intubation tube. It's like we've come a full circle, riding each curve of the road, through every trial and tribulation and now finally we are ending up where we began. Like all things, a beginning and an end.

Recovery "Sleepless Night," written on Tuesday, August 27th, 2013:

Here I am at 2:00 a.m., and I'm feeling wide awake. Have been since about 1:00 a.m., and before that, it was a restless kind of sleep. Beckett's heart rate was on the rise again last night around 8:00 p.m., and I knew his temperature must be rising. It was 100.2°, so we gave him some Tylenol and I tried to sleep, but instead found myself watching his heart rate on the monitor most of the night. He's kept a low-grade temperature all night/morning, along with the slightly elevated heart rate. I'm trying not to worry about this, but it's bothering me, especially since his blood tests yesterday were normal and he was on two antibiotics post-op for three days. In a way, I wish one of the tests would have shown something as it's a starting point to an answer of what is causing the changes. The unknown is frustrating. Time will tell, I suppose. And so, while I am wide awake sitting on my little sleeping couch next to the window, Beckett has been resting peacefully most of the night. I don't believe they have rescued him at all, and besides the elevated temperature/heartrate, all other stats look good. It's weird, because while I haven't left Beckett's side except for maybe ten to fifteen minutes in days, I still feel like I haven't seen him in a long time and am missing him dearly. He's normally such a busy, funny and sweet little boy, and since arriving at pre-surgery last Friday, I have yet to see that little boy again. The crazy thought has crossed my mind more than once: is this worth it? Is it worth putting Beckett through all of this for the outcome? What will the outcome be? Of course, it will be worth it in the very end, but in the midst of sleep deprivation, stress and the unknown, you start to wonder.

Recovery Post Operation Day 4, "Eureka & the OR," written on Tuesday, August 27th, 2013:

Eureka! We've got poop!

I am so happy to announce that around 4:00 a.m. this morning, Beckett finally pooped! I had fallen back asleep but told the night nurse to please wake me up if Beckett passed stool. Low and behold, a little after 4:00 a.m., she did, and let me tell you, it was quite a poop! I didn't care that it was 4:00 a.m. and he had just demolished his bed with crap; it was a glorious moment! Thank goodness. Beckett's got to be feeling better. His belly is still slightly distended, but much better than before. For the rounds this morning, there were no changes made as the ICU team was tentatively waiting for Beckett's bronchoscopy at 1:30 p.m. to decide the next course of action. Beckett did go NPO (turned off oral feeds) at 2:00 a.m. in preparation for his trip to the operating room. The only other update is that Beckett's chest X-ray this morning did seem to show more collapse than yesterday. Not enough for major concern, but something to continue to track. Also, the blood cultures did not come back as growing anything, which is a good sign. We have no idea why Beckett had a low-grade temperature and slightly elevated heartrate. Maybe just from surgery and/or the medications . . . My theory? It was the poop! Shortly before 1:30 p.m., the anesthesiologist and a nurse anesthetist came to Beckett's room to transport him from the ICU to the operating room. We were able to walk with them and our nurse for the day down to the operating room area. I kissed Beckett goodbye, and then my mom and I headed to the surgery waiting room. Theresa, who manages the waiting room, and now knows us and Beckett by name greeted us. Comforting, and a sign you've been through surgery too many times, I suppose. A little after 2:15 p.m., Dr. Jacobs came into the waiting area to speak with us. I was on edge, honestly not expecting great news, but Dr. Jacobs advised that the graft looks great and it's already starting to heal over. He said the plan would be to stop Beckett's current infusions of sedatives at 4:00 a.m. and also start propofol at the same time. Propofol is still a sedative, but it's much shorter acting. It will allow us to keep Beckett calm and not pulling out his tube before everyone is ready. And so today wasn't just a good day, it was a *great* day! Beckett pooped, and we received great news that he is on track for his real decannulation tomorrow. Can't ask for much more right now. Tomorrow will be a big day, like probably the biggest ever. It will be the first time since being born that Beckett will not be relying on something to help him breathe, like a baby bird leaving the nest for the first time. Tomorrow we will pull his breathing tube, pushing him out of the nest . . . Can't wait to watch him fly!

Recovery Post Operation Day 5, "Extubation & Withdrawal," written on Wednesday, August 28th, 2013:

First and foremost, Beckett is flying!

We still have a way to go before we are anywhere close to being back to ourselves, but he is finally tube free.

At 2:00 a.m., we turned off Beckett's feeds, and at around 3:45 a.m., we stopped Beckett's current sedation and started propofol. Since it's an anesthetic, a doctor had to come administer it, along with any changes in dosing. We did end up increasing it twice before extubation, but never to the full dosing we could have.

We were told 9:00 a.m. would be the magical time. By 8:45 a.m., I was pacing Beckett's room. A little after 9:00 a.m., the team arrived, and we started setting up and ensuring that everyone was ready. The propofol was stopped, and the feeding tube in Beckett's nose was pulled. Slowly Beckett started to wake, and thankfully he was quite calm. His eyes scanned the room and then would close and open slowly. I'm sure, to him his eyelids felt like the weight of the world rested on them. When everyone was ready, they started to remove the tape from each of Beckett's cheeks. He, of course, hated every minute of it, but was again quite still and calm. Then on the count of three, the intubation tube was slowly pulled from Beckett's nose. I wish I could say it was a peaceful and beautiful moment, but honestly, I was scared to death. I could feel my heart racing in my throat as I held my breath. The next moments were terrifying. Beckett started to cough and then vomited. They, of course, suctioned him out and, once clear, administered a breathing treatment via a mask. Once that was through, they placed Beckett on a nasal cannula with 6-liter flow and 40 percent oxygen. Over the next ten to fifteen minutes, Beckett continued to cough and vomit clearing mucus from his throat and upper airway. After about thirty minutes post extubation, Beckett was finally looking better. I felt like I was in heart failure.

The remainder of the morning and afternoon, we have remained on edge. Beckett's stats look good, as does a blood gas report that was done approximately an hour post extubation. However, Beckett is experiencing major withdrawal symptoms from all the pain and sedation medication that he has been on for the past week or so. All day he has been shaking, sweating and vomiting. It's awful and frightening. We've been giving him Tylenol and Zofran to help, but unfortunately, his symptoms are severe enough so we had to give him half of a rescue dose to help him. It's highly likely that we will have to wean him off over the coming days/potentially weeks from the medications he was on.

This afternoon, a very welcome guest stopped by. His name was Deuce. He has brown hair and was sporting a blue scarf. Deuce was a therapy dog. Normally, Beckett's face would have lit up and he would have been thrilled to see Deuce. Unfortunately, he is so sick he didn't even smile. Nevertheless, Deuce seemed to help me relax for just a minute with his deep brown eyes and silky-smooth coat. I sure hope he or another one of his "Paw Partners" will stop by again once Beckett is back to his usual self.

Earlier this afternoon, I was able to hold Beckett for the first time since last Friday. It felt good to have him in my arms, but I realized from getting him out of bed just how weak he is. He's like a rag doll. Tomorrow, occupational therapist, speech therapist and physical therapist are all coming to see Beckett. Most of them stopped by today to see him, but he is in no way ready today. We are also hoping tomorrow that he can start trying to eat orally. Since they pulled his feeding tube this morning, he will continue to receive fluids via his IV. Probably a good thing given the frequent vomiting and loss of fluids.

All in all, today was probably the most stressful and mentally exhausting. I am still on edge about Beckett as he is still "pulling" air at his neck when he breathes and will occasionally drop his oxygen saturation rates. So far so good, but I am realizing today that the road before us is still very, very long.

Recovery Post Operation Day 6, "Wired & Withdrawal," written on Thursday, August 29th, 2013:

I am too tired to journal a lengthy update tonight, but Beckett continues to struggle with withdrawal from his meds. At rounds this morning, they actually ended up adding scheduled doses of two different medications back in for Beckett to help him with the withdrawal symptoms. It's so crazy how much drugs seriously mess up your body. Anyone thinking about using drugs should watch someone go through withdrawal; it's one of the most awful things to witness. For Beckett, it starts with body tremors. His body shakes uncontrollably. Then he becomes super fidgety and his skin sweaty and clammy; it's like he is crawling out of his skin. That is usually followed by wrenching. Beckett has nothing to throw up, except the occasional stomach vial. Oh yeah, and Beckett has really bad diarrhea, and his eyes are constantly dilated. His episodes are usually about every four hours now, but yesterday were much more frequent. By last night, when he had an episode, I would get the nurse and have to leave the room. I couldn't take it anymore. I feel so helpless.

On a positive note, I do feel like today was better than yesterday in terms of the withdrawal, but we've still got a way to go, and by a way, I mean it could be that we are weaning Beckett off the meds for weeks. Right now, we really need the withdrawal symptoms to subside as they are really hindering recovery as Beckett will not eat and has no energy/motivation to play. Another side effect of the withdrawal is that Beckett is wired. He really only slept maybe two hours last night and then maybe an hour today. Poor guy. We are hoping for a more restful night tonight. Finally, to end on a high note, today we were able to wean Beckett off 6 liters and 30 percent oxygen on a high flow cannula to absolutely nothing. Finally, that beautiful little face and neck are completely *free*. More updates tomorrow, but for tonight, we both need rest.

Good night.

Recovery Post Operation Day 7, "Drooling & Progress," written on Friday, August 30th, 2013:

Knock on wood, I believe that we finally have Beckett's withdrawal under control. In fact, so much so that we weaned off one of the medications today altogether and are planning on lowering the dosing of the other one starting tonight.

Our other goal for the day was getting out of bed and get moving and to try to start eating. Speech, occupational and physical therapist came by yesterday, but B just stared at them with his blank sad eyes. Today, I am proud to say Beckett did much better at least with the occupational and physical therapist. The therapist had Beckett sitting up and going for wagon rides as well as trying to make some window art with crayons. And amazingly, Beckett walked (with support) "the bridge" today that connects two buildings. Incredible when a day ago he could not even bear weight on his legs. Speech is working on Beckett's eating, which, thus far, is not happening. Beckett is drooling really bad, which is generally a sign that either he is in pain when swallowing or not sure how to do it yet with the new airway. Thus, we really need Beckett to start eating. This is really the next hurdle to overcome and would put us a step closer towards discharge.

Recovery Post Operation Days 8 & 9, "Stronger & Swallowing," written on Sunday, September 1st, 2013:

Well, I had been trying to update my journal each night, but last night I was too tired to do so. Yesterday was a day spent with visitors. My dad is here this weekend, and then yesterday, Ryan's mom drove over from New Freedom, Pennsylvania, where she was visiting friends.

Beckett has continued to make progress on all fronts over the past two days. He is now completely off of the narcotics, and we have been able to keep his pain under control using just Tylenol. He's also been able to maintain his respiratory stats on just room air. In addition, Beckett continues to regain his muscle strength. He can now sit up on his own and just this morning was finally really close to being stable enough on his feet to walk without someone supporting him.

Swallowing continues to be our biggest hurdle. We have made significant progress over the past two days in that Beckett is eating ten to fifteen small spoonfuls of pudding/ice cream three to four times a day. My heart breaks for him, though, in that he is *so* hungry and wants to eat, but it takes him a good ten to fifteen minutes to get over the pain and start eating. He is still really drooling, again a sign that it's likely too painful to swallow. A speech therapist has been coming every day, even over the weekend to work with B. Unfortunately, they want him to "master" the soft solids before moving on. This afternoon when the speech therapist came, he didn't want to eat anything, pudding or milk. After they left, my dad came back with some BBQ from a local place down the street from the hospital. Beckett was dying for some French fries that he saw us eating. And so, even though not "approved" for him, we gave him some small soft pieces to see if he would be able to get over his pain. Sure enough, twenty French fries and some milk and cookies later, he was over it and talking up a storm! Since decannulation, we haven't heard anything from Beckett, but today he really opened up and started babbling and trying to talk to us. He would call us "Mama" and "Dada" and point and try to communication about the cars and trucks outside his hospital window. What a delight to hear! Tomorrow morning the speech therapist is coming again. I know they have their protocol and processes, but Beckett will never be a soft solid eater. Time to break the news to them so we can get out of here sooner than later!

At rounds this morning, there was talk about being moved from the ICU to the surgery recovery floor, but after speaking with ENT, it sounds like we will remain here until at least Tuesday. Honestly, I am good with that. While the ICU is busier and louder, the staff is ten times better here. At least that was our experience last fall. So, all in all, today was a really great day! Special thanks to nurse Grandpa who came this weekend to keep things "lively" and push the limits in Beckett's healing. *We love you, Dad!*

Recovery Post Operation Day 10, "Eating & Fluids," written on Monday, September 2nd, 2013:

Just a quick update for the day. Beckett has been cleared with an unlimited diet, with the restriction of the items being soft. So, for breakfast, pancakes and hash browns, for lunch, pizza. Slowly he is getting back to himself. At the rounds, the only change was to reduce his IV fluids to try to increase his desire to drink more. So, we are chugging right along. It was raining here this morning, so we weren't able to go outside with Beckett, but did go for a wagon ride/walk through the lobby and cafeteria. This afternoon we might try to get back outside since it's finally sunny out.

In other news, we are *so* glad that the menu in the cafeteria has finally changed. They have had the same thing since we were admitted, and given that cafeteria food isn't always the greatest, when there is limited variety, it's even worse. We've been getting takeout at some area restaurants, but it's pricey, not to mention what sounds the best right now is a home-cooked meal. Soon, hopefully, we will be able to be discharged. Should have a better idea tomorrow.

Recovery Post Operation Day 11, "Pulmonary Floor & Big Day Tomorrow," written on Tuesday, September 3rd, 2013:

Today was another great day of progress for Beckett. He was discharged from both occupational and physical therapies since he is almost back to his baseline in terms of gross and fine motor skills. He's still a bit unbalanced at times but can now walk on his own and do the stairs with help. He continued to eat and drink well yesterday and this morning, so during the rounds this morning, the IV fluids were stopped, and by noon, they had pulled his PICC line. Yay for no more dragging the IV pole around! Also, during rounds, they discussed, with ENT team's blessing, moving us from the ICU to the pulmonary floor. There was some delay as Beckett technically is still categorized as having a critical airway, and generally kids with that label must stay in the ICU, but after the ENT team explained Beckett's condition (post LTR surgery), they agreed to take him. We are basically being "observed" for one night, and then assuming all goes well tonight, we will be discharged tomorrow! *Yahoo!* Can't wait to get out of the hospital and finally be able to get a good night's sleep. Going on night #12 of interrupted sleep!

Recovery Post Operation Day 12, "Discharge & Sinking In," written on Wednesday, September 4th, 2013:

Beckett had another great night. With the exception of waking shortly after 10:00 p.m., he slept soundly the remainder of the night even through his 12:00 a.m. and 4:00 a.m. vital checks. His oxygen saturation rates were awesome, generally 97 to 100 percent most of the night. I know this because I have been awake since about 1:00 a.m. I think it finally started to sink in that we were leaving the hospital today *and* we were leaving the hospital without a trach. Thus far, I haven't felt like I have been able to enjoy and celebrate this milestone given that we were always working on some new goal to get discharged, but today those goals are met and we are finished. I have dreamed of this day for so long: no more lugging around the suction machine; no more trach care, which I estimate I have done around seven hundred times with a hundred trach changes; no more medical supplies in Beckett's closet; no more stares from strangers in public. Nope, a new adventure really does begin today. Beckett will soon be able to go swimming at the pool, play in the sand at the beach, attend preschool and so many other things that have not been possible in his life since birth. As I laid awake last night, I couldn't help but flash back to so many moments over the past thirty-one months: Beckett's early arrival and being so afraid of losing him, being transferred to Children's Mercy and finding out Beckett would need a trach, our first trach cares and changes while Beckett was still at Children's Mercy, finally being able to bring him home and literally having a hospital room in our living room. I can remember feeling isolated and frustrated by all of Beckett's medical equipment when taking Beckett along with me for runs while on his ventilator and to friends' houses for summer BBQs, feeling overjoyed when he was off the ventilator and then feeling absolutely devastated when we learned about his damaged airway, sending Beckett off to the OR more times than I can count, our first trip out here to Philadelphia, meeting Dr. Jacobs and the entire airway team here at CHOP, being homesick and feeling so far away but knowing in the back of our minds we were exactly where we were supposed to be. What an odyssey we have been on, and what a story Beckett will be able to tell someday.

This morning, the sun is shining and not a cloud in the sky is visible. It's a beautiful day to start a brand-new life for Beckett. Right now, the focus is getting Beckett out of here. For whatever reason, being discharged from the hospital always feels like we are running for the doors before someone can change their mind. And after twelve nights inpatient, this mama is not staying even a moment longer.

*End of journal entries

Once we were finally out those doors, we loaded up the car and headed to the Ronald McDonald House. We packed up there and then hit I-95 South to Bear, Delaware. My parents, amazing friends and old neighbors, Peggy and Dave, were once again gracious enough to open their home to us. This saved us so much, not just in accommodation expenditures, but to be in a home setting that was germ free while remaining on the East Coast until Beckett could be cleared to travel home was everything.

The last leg of the journey

Once settled in Delaware, our first order of business was catching up, catching up on sleep and rest and honestly just getting back to "normal," if there is such a thing in the world of having a medically compromised child. But for us, it meant sleeping in a room with no alarms or nurses, showering or bathing in a real bathroom, regaining our strength, getting on a more regular schedule, continuing to eat well and, of course, staying healthy so that Beckett's airway could continue to heal. My mom continued to stay with Beckett and I in Delaware since Ryan was still traveling back and forth for work.

After a week or so, we were feeling more normal and so took advantage once again of being on the East Coast by going and seeing what we could while still being very, very cautious of potential germ exposure for Beckett. Most of our outings were outdoors: local parks, visiting the Amish villages/towns, the Philadelphia zoo, riding the Cape May Ferry boat to see the Cape May Light House and even sneaking in "A Day Out with Thomas the Train" since Beckett was infatuated with trains. And although we were sanitizing fools while in public, it was a little taste of what life would be like once we were fully cleared, and it felt amazing.

I do remember on those first few outings feeling like I was always forgetting something. After hauling the suction machine and emergency trach bag for so many years, my arms felt empty with only a diaper bag. And my heart leaped each time I would see Beckett's neck without a trach or hear him try to mimic what we were saying and seeing on our outings. I think one of the greatest moments we had while waiting to be cleared to return home, was when we were able to take Beckett to the beach in New

Jersey near Cape May. Sand and water are two things that you don't do with a trach, or at least not with a toddler with a trach. But now we were free. We could walk through the sand and put our feet in the water. And that was exactly what we did. And Beckett must have felt this freedom, because he would hold fistfuls of sand, lay in the sand, throw the sand and then charge towards the water where I would chase after him to save him from the crashing waves. Needless to say, it was the most freeing moment we had while on the East Coast, and that door to the other side of a trach-free life was open almost completely now. We were so ready for it.

On September 12th, we returned to CHOP just for a clinic visit. And besides listening to Beckett, checking his ears and his incision sites, that was about it. I did sign off on the paperwork for Beckett to have his first bronchoscopy since decannulation, which was scheduled for September 20th. Depending on how things looked during that bronchoscopy, they would determine when we would be able to return home to Kansas City.

On Friday, September 20th, Mom and I once again drove to CHOP and arrived at same-day surgery. Ryan would be flying to Philadelphia later that day and meeting us at CHOP. We went through the same pre-surgery process that we had already been through countless times before. And shortly after 10:30 a.m., Beckett was taken back to the operating room. While I was waiting, a staff member from the hospital came to have me complete admission paperwork. If Dr. Jacobs needed to dilatate Beckett's airway or another intervention was needed, Beckett would likely be admitted to the ICU post-surgery. I remember praying silently in my head as I completed each form and initial box and the final signature line, *Please, please, please let us not be admitted back into the hospital.* No sooner had I surrendered the forms over to the hospital staff member than I looked up to see Dr. Jacobs in the waiting area looking for me. Thankfully, he smiled and said everything looked great before he even reached where I was sitting, maybe a sign that my face revealed what my mind was actually thinking. What a relief. I couldn't believe it. Everything looked perfect. Beckett's airway was healed. We could go home—home.

I sat for a moment processing everything. It was *over*. It was *finally over*: no more trach, medical equipment, surgeries, special care, in-home nursing, no more of so much that had made Beckett's life since birth anything but normal. No sir. The next day, we would board a plane back to Kansas City, trach free. I felt the burn and then blurry vision as tears filled my eyes and streamed down my face. What a feeling. Ryan arrived and met my mom and me in the post-surgery recovery area. Once Beckett was cleared from there, we left CHOP and headed towards Delaware where we packed up our things in preparation for our homecoming.

A
LONG-AWAITED
DESTINATION

Upon arriving home, one of the first things I did was pull all of the medical supplies out of Beckett's room. Of course, there were so many more important things I should have done first, but I couldn't wait to turn his room into a normal toddler's room. Ironically, we had received a letter from the medical supply company while we were in Delaware notifying us that we were now the "owners" of the suction machine and pulse oxygen machine. I guess after your insurance rents them year after year and you pay enough money, you eventually own the things. So many times, Ryan and I wanted to set-fire to the suction machine as it was so loud and we were so tired of lugging it everywhere, and now here we were, the owners of it! I called the medical supply company, and a few days later, they came by to pick up all of Beckett's extra supplies and oxygen tanks. And while I was ready to trash all the remaining stuff, I did save some of Beckett's old trachs in his "Baby Keepers" container; after all, they are part of his story.

On October 2nd, 2013, we returned to the Children's Mercy Hospital special care clinic for our final appointment with them. We had been going to the special care clinic since Beckett was discharged from CMH in May of 2011. Of all of our experiences with CMH, some good and some bad, I have nothing but wonderful things to say about the clinic. The main doctors (neonatologist) who specialize in at-home trach and ventilating kiddos are amazing, especially Dr. Linda Gratney. I cannot say enough about her expertise with trach kiddos, commitment to her patients and her wonderful bedside manners.

I can remember many times calling the twenty-four-hour hotline in the middle of the night when Beckett was sick and being connected with Dr. Gratney on the other end of the line. She was always calm and cool and gave us ventilator adjustments and inhaler dosing to help Beckett get through the night and remain at home instead of a trip to the emergency room and admission to the ICU. In addition—and why she will always hold a very special place in my heart—Dr. Gratney willingly took on our insurance company in the fight to provide Beckett with in-home nursing care when the company denied our claims. She provided them with industry practices and research for trach children at home, she attended conference calls with the case management company and in the end was right there on the front lines with me, advocating for what we knew was needed not just for Beckett, but for other kids like Beckett who might need in-home nursing care in the future. And in the end . . . we won! Our insurance company now offers in-home nursing care for trach- and ventilator-dependent children who are able to remain at home. Dr. Gratney was supportive in our decision to seek a second opinion at CHOP for Beckett's airway reconstruction. She helped to ensure that we had everything we needed with our medical records, getting appointments for testing prior to a surgery and acted as a sounding board for any questions and concerns I wanted to validate.

The appointment was bittersweet. On one side, I was overjoyed that Beckett was well enough that we no longer need to go to Children's Mercy Hospital for care, but on another, I knew I would miss the doctors and not being able to call at any time of day their emergency number and be connected to the experts who had known Beckett nearly his entire life. Once we wrapped up the actual appointment, we took a few pictures with Beckett and the clinic care team. Then Dr. Gratney and

Dr. Lachica wanted to take Beckett on a little tour around the hospital. First, we went to the offices that house many of the NICU doctors and staff. It was so great to see many of the neonatologists who took care of Beckett when he was inpatient at Children's. They couldn't believe how great Beckett looked, and I could see the reward on their faces of seeing a once really sick baby boy who was now a completely healthy and happy toddler. Next, we went to the actual NICU floor. Upon entering the NICU, tears filled my eyes. I had not been back to the NICU since we were discharged, and something about the lights and the smell brought back very raw memories of many times before when I had walked through those secure doors, exhausted, emotionally drained and many times hopeless. We walked through Pod A, which was where Beckett's bed was, A5 and A3 to be exact. It looked the same, as did many of the nurses who also couldn't believe how great Beckett looked and what a doll he was. So many of them made the comment that it meant *so* much that we came back to visit as they never get to see the end result and how these once tiny babies end up happy and healthy kids. I think it's safe to say Beckett was the sunshine in quite a few people's day during our tour.

Finally, and what really brought everything full circle for me was when we rounded a corner and I saw Tracy. If you remember, Tracy was a NICU nurse at Saint Luke's Hospital where I delivered Beckett. She was actually at my delivery and took care of Beckett in the first minutes of his life and for the first four days in the NICU post birth. She was also there the first time we tried to extubate Beckett at Saint Luke's (prior to a trach) when Beckett coded. She took care of Beckett multiple times in those early days when he was so sick. And when we were transferred to Children's Mercy, she came to visit Beckett and us at the hospital on her off days. She was one of the truly amazing nurses we met along this journey. Shortly after we were transferred to Children's, Tracy went back to school to become a neonatal nurse practitioner at Children's, which was where she was on that day.

When I saw Tracy, it felt like I had closed my eyes and a highlight reel was running of our entire journey: Beckett being born early, those terrifying early days when he was so fragile, the ups and downs of the NICU, his heart surgery, growth and weight gain, almost reaching extubation, coding, multiple diagnoses of his airway, transfer to CMH, getting his trach, learning all about caring for trachs, coming home on a ventilator, in-home nurses, fighting with the insurance company, multiple therapy interventions, second opinions, CHOP, Dr. Jacobs, trips to the operating room, traveling to Philadelphia with Beckett for care, surgeries, surgeries and more surgeries, painful recoveries . . . and finally here we were. We were on the other side, the side with none of that anymore. That door that was closed for so long and then tempted us by cracking open, we had finally walked through. This was it. We had made it to Italy.

Only now that I was on the other side looking back could I see our long journey in a different light. While the pain and heartache would always remain, something else shined brighter now. Instead of seeing so much hardship when I look back on our journey with Beckett, I can now see the profound love that carried us through every trial and tribulation: the love of my parents to their daughter and grandson; the love of the doctors and nurses who chose a profession because they love it and that love helped to heal, treat and ultimately save Beckett; the love of fellow parents whom I met along the way, all of us fighting the hardest fight, but silently cheering on those who were walking with us through the pain and loss; the love of a community of friends and coworkers and neighbors and sometimes complete strangers who offered kind words, home-cooked meals and money to help get us through; the love of a spouse who when tested with "for better or worse" hung on tight and refused to give up on each other; and ultimately, my love for my first born, Beckett. My love cared, comforted, nursed and fueled him to keep going, to try to walk, to try to talk, to try to eat, to try to breathe and do all the things we needed him to do. And when I was tired, it was the love around me that filled me up and kept me going, even when it all seemed impossible. And isn't that what they always teach you?

"Amour vincit Omnia, et nos cedamus amori" —Virgil ("Love conquers all things, so we too shall yield to love.")

On a road we did not choose and a path that awarded no mercy, it was truly love that carried us to our final destination.

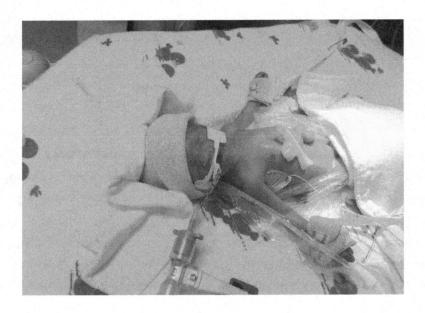

January 2, 2011, Beckett shortly after being born at St. Luke's Hospital.

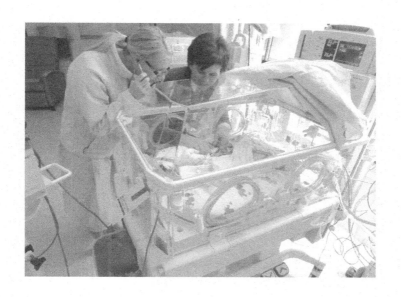

January 2, 2011, learning about preemie care
from Beckett's NICU nurse that day, Tracy.

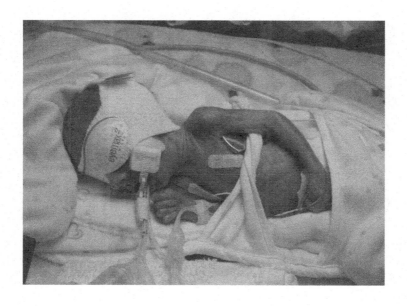

January 6, 2011, Beckett in the incubator under the bilirubin light.
His weight this day was 800 grams.

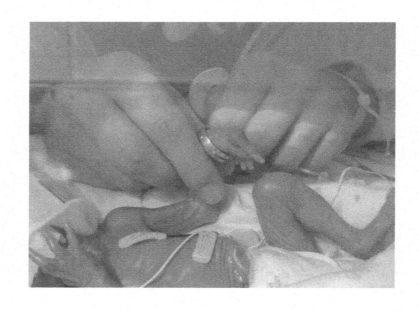

Ryan's wedding ring on Beckett's tiny arm.

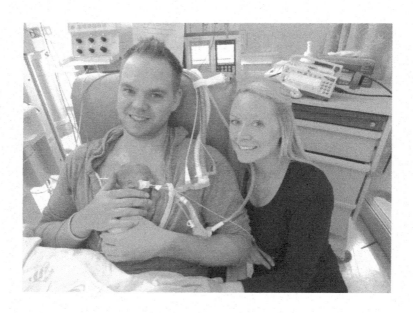

January 22, 2011, the first time Ryan was able to hold Beckett at St. Luke's Hospital.

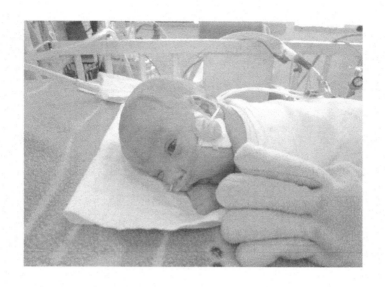

March 21, 2011, the start of Beckett's trial on nasal cannula which ended with a transfer to Children's Mercy Hospital.

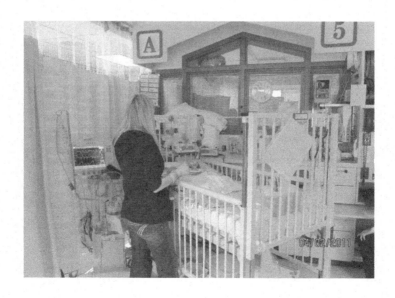

April 2011, one of the first days after Beckett received his trach at Children's Mercy Hospital.

April 2011, the first smile after healing from trach
surgery at Children's Mercy Hospital.

My Mom at Children's Mercy Hospital with Beckett during the time
when she came to help keep him on track for discharge.

May 31, 2011, a family photo as we were leaving the NICU
at Children's Mercy Hospital after 150-days inpatient.

May 31, 2011, Beckett all smiles driving away from Children's Mercy
Hospital to go home for the first time since being born.

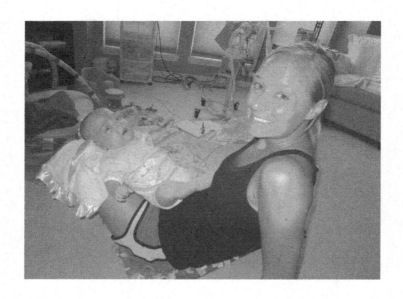

July 2011, life at home with Beckett. This photo was taken in our living room which was also his bedroom at the time.

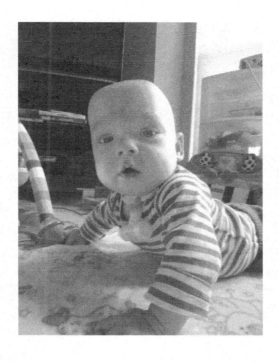

October 2011, Beckett was 10-months old
and was off the ventilator and working on pushing up.

January 2, 2012, Beckett's first birthday.

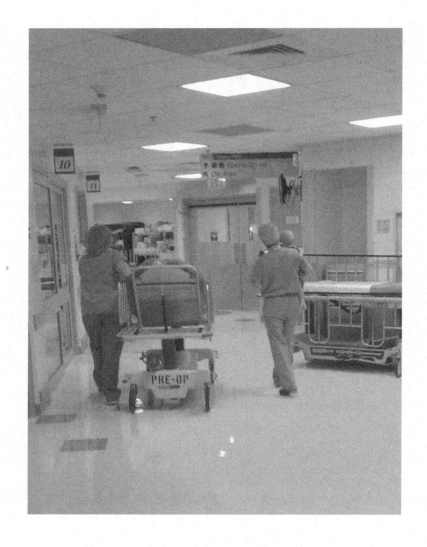

April 2012, two nurses carry Beckett through the infamous
Children's Hospital of Philadelphia surgery doors.

April 2011, our initial consult at the Children's Hospital
of Philadelphia for Beckett's airway diagnosis.

August 2012, my Dad, at our home, helping to nurse Beckett back
to health after his Tonsil and adenoid removal.

August 2012, family pictures before Beckett's first LTR surgery.

October 2012, Beckett recovering in the PICU at the Children's Hospital of Philadelphia post his double stage LTR surgery.

**October 2012, wagon rides with Beckett, "The Mayor"
of the PICU at the Children's Hospital of Philadelphia.**

**October 2012, Beckett recovering with a therapy dog after his double
stage LTR surgery at the Children's Hospital of Philadelphia**

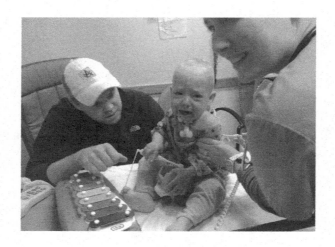

October 2012, Beckett in the pre-operative area before one of his many broncoscopies at the Children's Hospital of Philadelphia.

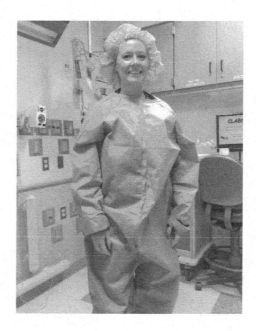

December 2012, Natalia in her "bunny suit" to walk Beckett back to surgery at the Children's Hospital of Philadelphia.

August 2013, "The Dream Team", Rosemary Patel-NP, Natalia, Beckett and Dr. Ian Jacobs at the Children's Hospital of Philadelphia.

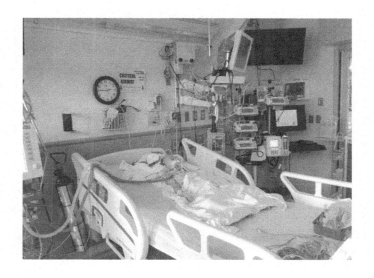

August 2013, Beckett in PICU at the Children's Hospital of Philadelphia immediately after his single stage LTR surgery.

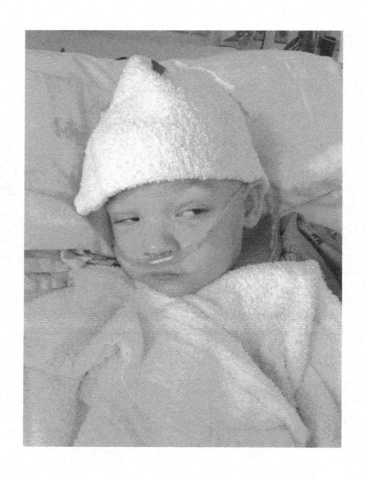

August 2013, Beckett post extubation from his single stage LTR surgery and struggling with withdrawal symptoms.

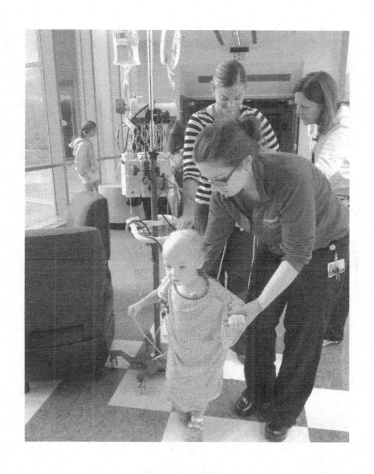

August 2013, Beckett learning to walk again with the help
of therapist at the Children's Hospital of Philadelphia.

September 2013, Beckett starting to come back to himself after some French Fries from my Dad.

September 2013, Cape May, New Jersey. Beckett was
"free at last" from needing any medical assistance to breathe.

Ryan, Beckett, Natalia and Peggy and Dave in front of Peggy
and Dave's home in Bear, Delaware, where they were able to stay while
Beckett was recovering from his LTR surgeries.

October 2013, The Children's Mercy Hospital Home Ventilator Team on Beckett's final visit post decannulation.

October 2013, Beckett with Tracy, Nurse Practitioner, at Children's Mercy Hospital, on his final visit post decannulation.

AFTERWORD

This book came to life after much encouragement from my grandmother, Phyllis Kist. It was something I always had on my to-do list, but when I sat down to write, I struggled to mentally go back and revisit many of the trials of Beckett's journey. Some were so dark I am pretty sure that I lost the key to that compartment in my mind altogether. That was likely why it took me nearly eight years to finally write it to its completion.

My intent for this book was to share the day-to-day trials of having a premature baby, the emotional toll of seeking care for a medically compromised child and, more specifically, the process of seeking a medical second option, traveling for medical care and the recovery process after a LTR surgery. Ryan and I still participate periodically in calls with other parents from CHOP who are considering or facing a LTR for their children, or parents of newly born premature babies. If I could have had such a reference book for those early days in the NICU or as we navigated our way through second opinions and LTR surgeries, it would have been amazing. Not just from an informational standpoint, but also to know that I wasn't alone in my feelings as I walked through our trials.

So, if that is you, I hope you found this book helpful. Or maybe you are walking through another trial in life, and if so, I hope that in this book you find hope and love and are able to reflect back on those in your personal journey.

Beckett is now a healthy eleven-year-old boy who enjoys playing cello, golfing and Legos. Thankfully, he has had no additional setbacks with regards to his airway being rebuilt and no need for additional medical care stemming from being born a preemie and having such a rough start at life.